INSIDE ALLEGANY

Volume II

2

TO MY SONS
TECK, JESS AND NICK
BEAHAN

INSIDE ALLEGANY

Volume II

LARRY BEAHAN

COYOTE PUBLISHING OF WESTERN NEW YORK
5 DARWIN DRIVE
SNYDER NEW YORK 14226
LARRY_BEAHAN@ROADRUNNER.COM

2012

COPYRIGHT 2012 LAURENCE T BEAHAN MD
ISBN 978-0-9703104-7-7

7

INSIDE ALLEGANY VOLUME II

CONTENTS

PART I: PEOPLE

MIDGE DEAN STOCK
SENECA TALES

BOB BYLEDBAL
MASTER OF THE REVELS

GEORGE HERON
ONE MORE STORY

LYN'S FIRST TRIPS
TO ALLEGANY STATE PARK

RICK FEUZ
AND HIS VOLUNTEERS

MERCY
KILLED TOOTS

GRACE CHRISTY
AND THE CCC

JOAN MILLIGAN
ALLEGANY COMMISSIONER

PART II: PASSIONS

BLACK BEARS
RICK ROTH

LOST
LARRY BEAHAN

SKIING IN ALLEGANY
SANDRA, LANCE AND LARRY ANDERSON

ALLEGANY MAMMALS
WAYNE ROBINS

SENECA SNOW SNAKE
MICHAEL KRAUSE

ALLEGANY SKI CHAMPION
EDNA NORTHRUP

PART III: PLACES

ALLEGANY AUTUMN
LARRY BEAHAN

A BRIEF HISTORY OF ALLEGANY STATE
PARK
BOB SCHMID

HELLBENDERS AND WALLEYES
SENECA NATION OF INDIANS FISH AND
WILDLIFE SERVICE

NEW YORK STATE FIRE TOWERS
PAUL LASKY

NEW IRELAND
PAUL LEWIS

TUNESASSA
CARL DEAN "PETE" SMALLBACK

PART IV: POLITICS

MINERAL RIGHTS SUNSET LAW
SIERRA CLUB'S MEMORANDUM OF
SUPPORT

A NEW ALLEGANY MASTER PLAN
SIERRA CLUB'S MEMORANDUM OF
SUPPORT

12

ACKNOWLEDGEMENTS

This two-volume book was made possible by the Allegany State Park Historical Society in its enthusiastic pursuit of old Allegany hands to relive Park history for us. The willingness of those Park denizens to tell their stories was the absolute essential ingredient. I wrote down what they had to say.

Thanks go to the Allegany State Park Administration for providing meeting space in the Red House Administration Building and the St. John's-in-the-Woods Chapel where these stories could be told in the setting of rustic cabins, rippling lakes and forested hills, where in fact they happened.

Photos were generously loaned by the Buffalo Museum of Science, Seneca Nation of Indians Fish and Wildlife Service, Buffalo State-Courier Express Collection, Bob Byledbal, Bob Schmid, John Phelps, Rick Feuz, Lyn Beahan, Wayne Robins, Edna Northrup, Sally Marsh, Ted LaCroix, Alfred Karney, Bruce Perry and Paul Lewis.

My sincerest thanks to you all.

Larry Beahan

INTRODUCTION

Inside Allegany is a collection of stories told by people who love Allegany State Park. They worked in the Park; played here, some were born here. The book is divided into two volumes simply because one would be too large. The division also serves to roughly divide the stories into earlier and later. Each volume has four parts: *People, Passions, Places* and *Politics*.

Allegany State Park is 60,000 acres in size and close to 100 years old. These two volumes give you only a glimpse at all that has gone on here.

PREVIEW VOLUME I

The *People* section of *Volume I* allows several Allegany characters to introduce themselves. George Heron worked with the Civilian Conservation Corps in the Park, later was elected president of the Seneca Nation, and led the Seneca protest against the Kinzua Dam. Hook France, a former Park Ranger, was born and still lives in the Park as is the case with Red House Town Justice Lance Anderson. I'll let you discover the other characters.

Passions refers not only to the many relationships that have blossomed in the Park including my wife Lyn and my honeymoon as camp counselors but also to all the varied activities people have loved doing here: ski-jumping and ski-racing, singing at Hootenannies and in choirs, telling stories around campfires, making maple syrup and, believe it or not, racing sport cars on frozen Red House Lake.

Places: The land comprising Allegany had a long history before it became a State Park. Fascinating remnants of that history are hidden in its forests and under its lakes, including cemeteries, building foundations and oil wells. Our steel Summit Fire Tower served to protect the Park for years but now, as a relic, it provides a wonderful view. And close by are the colorful nineteenth-century communities of Cattaraugus and Ellicottville.

Politics, many of us prefer to forget about politics when we escape into the woods. This section takes an opposite tack to look at threats to Allegany State Park and what we can do to protect the Park.

PREVIEW VOLUME II

The *People* section of the second volume of *Inside Allegany* begins with Seneca storyteller Midge Dean Stock. I love her story about how Rabbit got so ugly, especially since she admits it is hard to believe. Bob Byledbal ran concessions and dancehalls in the Park. Next time you see him, ask him to sing the Cornplanter song or if he really told his staff to tell customers, "Those are raisins, not flies, in the ice cream."

Mercy Holliday was a waitress at the Red House Inn. She tells the amazing story of her aunt's obedient pet turtle, Toots. Women are more evident in Volume II. That may justify the cover photo of campers in 1920's swimsuits at the old Quaker Run Mud Hole. I like to think of them as the Ziegfeld Follies Girls.

Passion: People are passionate about bears. Dick Roth covers black bears for us and naturalist Wayne Robins teaches us about the many other mammals encountered here including coyote, raccoon, beaver, fox, squirrel and the rare and vicious fisher, an animal that can spin around inside its own skin and bite an attacker. Seneca snow-snake-maker Michael Crouse initiates us into Snow Snake, a sport in which a stick is thrown at amazing speed and travels down an icy trough for a mile or more.

Places: Bob Schmid attempts a synopsis of the whole history of the Park. Pete Smallback takes us on a tour of a section of the Friends Boat Launch which used to be his family's farm and before that was Tunesassa, the Quaker Seneca Indian School. Paul Lewis leads us to the ruins of an Irish immigrant settlement in Red House. And the Seneca Fish and Wildlife Service show off their Steelhead Trout and Allegany Hellbender (giant salamander) rearing installations.

Volume II's *Politics* section brings us full circle. It describes the new Allegany State Park Master Plan signed into law in 2011 that protects the Park from lumbering and mineral extraction and guarantees that it will be there as we know it for a good long while.

Whatever your passions, I wish you a great time at Allegany, the best Park in the world.

PART ONE

PEOPLE

MIDGE DEAN STOCK
SENECA TALES

August 2004

That August day was bright and cool in Allegany State Park. It had rained much of the summer so the grass and woods were moist and green but brilliant in that sun of which we had seen so little. In preparation for an adventure in Seneca tradition, we propped open the shutters of the old Allegany-style cabin that serves as the St. John's-in-the-Woods Chapel.

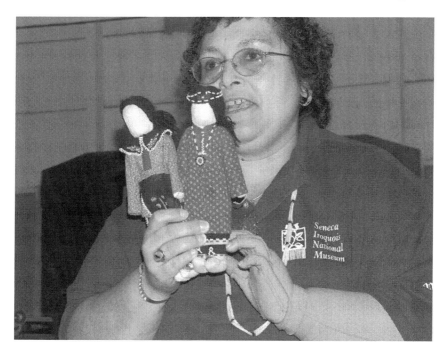

Midge Jean Stock 2004

Michelle, better know as Midge, Dean Stock came to sing songs and tell us stories. She belongs to the Wolf clan of the Senecas. Midge was born at Cold Spring on the Allegany Reservation. Her mother speaks all six of the Iroquois languages. Her brother, Robert Dean, is an anthropologist. She, herself, is an author and educator, has served as Director of Education for the Seneca Nation and Director of the Seneca National Museum in Salamanca.

Midge's Audience at St. John's-in-the-Woods

She is a robust, dark-haired woman whose voice in conversation is sometimes unexpectedly small and high-pitched but that day in the midst of song and story she filled the room with eloquence and held us in rapt attention. A silver Wolf Clan medallion, a turquoise bracelet, beadwork earrings and a shell necklace turned her maroon polo shirt labeled Seneca National Museum and black slacks into distinctive Seneca dress. A flesh-colored constricting bandage covered her left arm and hand. She had been ill but she insisted that she wanted to do this performance for us anyway. She certainly did not come across as ill that day.

I helped her carry a heavy basket from which she produced a collection of Seneca art. On the polished wooden box at the front of the chapel containing the artifacts used in Christian ritual, she laid a display that included horn and turtle rattles, a feathered headdress, faceless corn husk dolls, a water drum, a porcupine-quill decorated fan, her own brightly-beaded baby moccasins and a set of adult moccasins. She invited us all to come up, look at and handle these beautiful objects but asked us to be careful not to handle the turtle rattle.

Midge demonstrating Seneca Handiwork

I am not sure if that was because of special reverence for the turtle as a Seneca symbol of creation or because of its delicacy. I suspect it was not delicacy because she demonstrated how the rattle is used at a dance by shaking it really loud and smashing it down on the altar rail. The bang scared the *bejesus* out of me, for a second.

The Senecas are losing their language but Midge is doing her best to keep it alive. She gave us a traditional Seneca greeting which was a long way from our "Hello. How are you doing?"

Her greeting in Seneca probably took a full 45 seconds to deliver. Then she translated and I got down parts of it, "I'm thankful you are well. Thanks to the creator for this nice day and thanks for his gathering us together here today," and much more.

Next Midge picked up a cow horn rattle filled with cherry pits or popcorn and set a rhythmic beat as she sang a Seneca anthem. It was a stirring melodic piece not at all like the western movie chanting that Hollywood has made us accustomed to. She followed this with a slower, quieter more haunting song.

The Iroquois refer to themselves as Haudenosaunee or People of the Longhouse. They use their style of shelter to distinguish themselves from other tribes. Everyone living in a particular longhouse is descended from one woman except for the men. Men married into the longhouse from outside. Women owned the longhouse, appointed the chiefs.

Another form of relationship is by clan. There are ten Seneca clans and they are divided into earth creatures and air creatures.

In the old days stories were told in the longhouses but only during the winter. Midge said that was because the squirrels would stop to listen and not store up enough food for winter and the trees would not do their work nor would the people. The work of the world would stop while all listened. This kind of put me in mind of how I could never get our kids to do any cleaning up while the television was on and we had to set certain hours for TV so that homework would be taken care of.

Midge said that when she was a kid on the old Allegany Reservation before the flooding of Kinzua Reservoir, every

Saturday night they would come down to the longhouse which served as kind of a church and community center. Everyone brought a dish to pass. The elders would teach dancing and tell stories. She said, "They told really scary stories about monsters to keep kids from going off in the woods by themselves. I was too scared to go to the outhouse alone. And funny stories and stories to explain about history. Some of them were a little off color and there are young kids here so I can't tell them. It was a lot of fun, a social event."

Midge Chatting with Alice Altenburg

I'll have to say I was a little disappointed that we weren't going to get the full Seneca story treatment. But Midge then launched into the Seneca story of creation, which was pretty absorbing anyway. It went about like this:

At first all there was was water and sky. There were sky people who were a lot like us but they were different, too, like their children came more quickly. They had everything you could want, all kinds of delicious food. There was a sacred tree on which everything grew but no one was allowed to eat or hurt any part of that tree.

One sky woman was pregnant and like pregnant women do, she got a strange appetite. She wanted, no, she had to have, tea brewed from the root of that sacred tree. People objected and told her that was against the rules but she found a place to hide among the roots of this big old tree and began digging. She wanted really tender roots from deep down. As she dug further and further into her pit, it opened a hole in the bottom of the sky. Bits of earth started falling through. The hole opened wider and wider. She started sliding through it. She screamed and tried to hold on to roots and earth. No one would help. Some say that her husband even kind of kicked her down a little. She lost her grip and fell screaming and thrashing down through the hole in the sky.

Below, the water animals saw her and heard her crying, "Help!" The birds got together under her as she fell and tried to make a blanket of their wings to catch her. But it didn't work, she fell on through. They yelled to the turtle and he came over, got under her and broke her fall. So there she was, sitting on a turtle, surrounded by nothing but water and she cried. She wailed, "I'll never see my folks again. I'm going to die."

The water animals felt very sorry for her and tried to console her. Several of them dove down to the bottom of the water to try to bring up mud to mix with the bit of earth that had fallen with her onto the turtle's back but they drowned. Muskrat finally succeeded. Turtle grabbed it from him and packed it on his back. . The woman put the two muds together and danced on them. Out of these two bits of earth the world began to form and she had a place to live.

Soon her baby was born, a daughter. The girl grew very, very quickly. A man with two arrows across his chest came along. They liked each other and soon she was pregnant. But it was a troublesome pregnancy, a pair of twins who were exact opposites, one left-handed the other right, one good, the other evil. They began fighting even while in their mother's womb. (I am listening to Midge's story and suddenly I am reminded of our kids again. But these twins were much worse.)

The good twin was born first and in the normal way. The other one was so contrary that he refused to follow his brother's route. Instead he found a spot where his mother's skin was thinnest and worked his way out there, right under her arm pit. His contrariness killed his own mother.

The sky woman, their grandmother, took care of the boys and she favored the left-handed evil one. They buried the boys' mother in the earth and from her sprouted the three sisters, corn, bean and squash. So the Senecas say these great sustaining foods come from their mother, the earth. Indian tobacco whose smoke carries prayers to the creator comes from the same source.

Between them the twins went on to create everything else in the world. And they fought as they created and still their grandmother favored the evil one. The right-handed twin made flowers and berries so the left-hander made brambles and thistles. The right-handed twin made poison and the contrary left-hander made cures which may seem out of character but it shows that no one is all good or all bad. The twins gave the Senecas lacrosse with its two opposing teams and the peach pit game where one side of the pit is burned and the other polished.

The twins battled and fought but they couldn't be killed. So eventually the left-handed one took over the dark, along with the devils. The right-handed one took the day but he was so angry at his grandmother's favoritism that he tore off her head and her head became the moon. She sometimes sneaks out during the day to see what the good twin is up to.

So that is how the world came to be.

"Now I'll tell you a silly story that is hard to believe," Midge said and it went about like this:

Rabbit was not very bright but he used to be a lot better looking than now. He used to have regular ears about like a dog's. His lip wasn't split. His front and hind legs were both about the same length; he had a nice big bushy tale and no buck teeth. One day late in summer he went wandering off singing and eating berries and he got pretty far from home. The other animals called to him. "What's wrong? You're far from home and you need to put away food for the winter." But he paid them no attention.

The skies were dark and fall came on. He kept eating and singing "I wish the sun would shine, I wish the sun would shine." He was so dumb. The snow came and he danced and laughed at the animals who taunted him. He caught snowflakes on his tongue. Food got scarce, the snow got deeper and deeper but all of a sudden he found a bush full of berries and leaves. He climbed into it and ate and ate and ate until he fell asleep. He slept and slept the longest time.

Water Drum

When he woke, the snow had melted and he discovered he wasn't in a bush at all but in the very top of a tall tree. He wasn't much of a climber and he was terrified. He tried to climb down and he fell head over heels whack, bang, bump.

One ear caught on a branch and got stretched and then the other. He landed in a crotch of a branch, one leg on one side, one on the other. He split his lip so his teeth showed. He bounced off, went into a dive and landed head first into the ground. Both his arms were out in front so they wound up short.

The creator never changed his looks back. He made the rabbit stay like that to remind people not to be dumb. The pussy willows are little bits of rabbit tail.
.

Young Girl from Audience with Midge's Dolls and Turtle Rattle

Midge took some more time before she closed to demonstrate how the water drum changes pitch when you add various amounts of moisture to the drum head. She showed us the faceless corn husk dolls and explained that only the creator could make a face. The buckskin and porcupine quill fan was decorated in a pattern of bright red wild strawberries. Midge said, "This gives thanks to the creator for earth, health and for feeding us. When you die you stay around the earth for ten days to finish up your business and to feast. These wild strawberries are what you eat along the path on your way."

She then sang us a song of farewell. When she finished she said, "It means. You, come again. We'll see you again…in this life or next.

She stayed on for another hour as children and adults piled around her asking questions and trying out rattles, drums and the headdress. I had a chance to ask her about the huge conglomerate boulder in front of the museum. I said rumor was that it had been used to grind arrowheads and make human sacrifices.

Midge said "We weren't much into human sacrifice. Only torture!"

We looked at the bowl carved in this rock and Midge said, "This probably was used to grind corn."

Just before she left someone asked her about ghosts over at Witch's Walk. "Witch's Walk," she said. "We call it Gahine. It is where you see the Gahi, those strange lights. You know once when I was in high school I saw High Hat. He is the one with the high hat like Abe Lincoln and bare feet. When I was in high school, two friends and I were coming home in a car late at night. And there he was, walking along the road by the twin bridges, where the longhouse used to be. I was so scared."

And she left us on that note. On my way home I looked carefully into the woods for one of those twins and crossing the Allegany on Route 86 I tried to spot where the longhouse might have been and watched warily out of the corner of my eye for High Hat.

29

BOB BYLEDBAL
MASTER OF THE REVELS

November 2008

Bob Byledbal, Allegany-raconteur-extraordinaire-bar-none, addressed the Historical Society in the Administration Building museum this rainy first-day-of-hunting season. The woods were full of armed men, the economy was in the midst of the worst recession since 1929 and we were happy to be indoors, warm and ready for entertainment.

Bob Byledbal, 2008

From 1958 to 1978 Bob ran all the concessions in Allegany State Park and before that he worked for his dad who ran them. The concessions included a dancehall and a combination restaurant-grocery store on each side of the Park, Red House and Quaker Run.

Bob is a big, jolly guy with a big voice and a big laugh. He looked prosperous in a new baseball cap, polo shirt, and chinos. Holding up a poster he had just purchased on E-bay, he said, "Most of you probably know, I've been in the car business and you know we are getting into some hard times. Well, we been there before," he said. By then I had read the antique poster:

1929 Ford Phaeton
Marked down
was $460, now $440

When the laughter quieted he waved to two, now middle-aged, men in the audience. "These two guys, Louis and Mark Klemann, worked for me in the store when they were kids." They stood up and grinned while we applauded.

Klemann Family in audience

Bob brought along home movies that his family had taken in the Park in the 1950's. Grace Christy had set them up on the museum projector so Bob could talk as she showed them. And did he talk. He kept up a running stream of anecdotes before, during and after the movies. To tell the truth, his anecdotes made a much greater impression on me than the movies. Don't get me wrong, the movies set a nice tone with flurries of 1950's cars, sun-tanned people in shorts, teens dancing, the inside of the Quaker Store and a memorable scene in the Rose Garden at Charlie Dach's Red House Inn during the annual Year-Rounders formal dinner.

Bob, Bill and Irene Byledbal at right, with Suppliers
Courtesy of Bob Byledbal

Here is a rough idea of what he had to say:

"While I had the concessions, there was a big turnaround, he said. "When I began, the Park was all nature and camping. It gradually got wild with beer and drugs. In the 1970s there were robberies, a motorcycle gang burned down a camp and the store got robbed.

"But before that we had wonderful times. Our 'Dawn Dances', the ones that went on till dawn, were the original Woodstock. We had cars backed up all the way from the Red House toll booths to the store. They drank so much beer that one time Dave Remington filled up his whole car with empties.

"The Red House store and dancehall were built in the Depression by the CCC (Civilian Conservation Corps). The dance floor we had was one of the best in the country. It was waxed bird's-eye maple built on top of the concrete floor of Al Sharp's barn. It never sank. We'd have 1500 people on it. The Quaker dancehall floor was on stilts. When we got 1500 on that one, it rocked.

Red House Store 1963
Courtesy Bob Byledbal

"I had an apartment with a view of the lake and the Red House Store. My parents had quarters over the Quaker Store which is now the Quaker Museum. They had a restaurant where the souvenir store is now. There was a juke box and a pool table. And then across the crick was the dancehall.

Bob Byledbal Red House Pavilion 1959
Courtesy of Bob Byledbal

We'd run a dance on one side of the Park one night and on the other side next night. They started out with square dances and then rock and roll came in with garage bands like "Iron Horse" and "Milk and Cookies." "Big Wheelie and the Hub Caps" became a national act. *"Cornplanter"* was an original of theirs." Bob rolled out his baritone:

"Cornplanter, Cornplanter
What can you do?
Now that there's
No longer Kinzu."

Here, Bob Schmid brought forward a little short senior citizen with a huge grin. He carried an antique poster announcing: "Joe Oliverio's Orchestra, Friday July 16 at Red House." The little guy pointed to the sign, "That's me!" And Bob said, "This is Joe Oliverio." Joe got a big hand.

Band Leader Joe Oliverio on left

Bob Byledbal shook hands with Joe, then he waved to Alice Altenberg in the audience. She smiled back demurely. "And Alice worked in Charlie Dach's restaurants. That makes five of us here today who worked in the Park in the1950's."

I'm not sure whether Blackie, the store dog, turned up in the movies or if someone asked about him. But Bob said, "Blackie was Bob Remington's dog. We took him over. He used to run to school and back with Dave Remington. My mother hated bugs and hated using the old outhouse. Blackie would run to the outhouse ahead of her and bark the bugs away. When we went home for the winter Blackie stayed in the Park. Pretty soon we got a call from the Park police. 'Blackie's running deer.' So we came down and got one of the Park workers, Hank, to take care of him. We left him a supply of dog food. Turned out, that Hank ate the dog food and Blackie ate Hank's baloney and mac.

"Our milk used to come in glass bottles from a Salamanca dairy. When I was thirteen or fourteen I wanted some practice driving so I backed the truck into the loading dock at the Quaker Store. I misjudged it, smacked into the dock and spilt cartons of milk all over. I went running for Mom.

Behind the Counter of Red House Store, 1960
Courtesy of Bob Byledbal

"I always liked driving cars. After we were married, I used to race stock cars. I'd be out hunting skunks and spinning around. I'd be two sheets to the wind. My wife would yell. Finally I got the car hung up. My wife said if I gave up racing I could buy a Corvette instead of new rugs for the house. That was '67. I just saw my old Corvette for sale on the internet for $60,000. Wonder what those rugs would be worth now?

"Outhouse T-shirts, we had T-shirts made up with an outhouse on them and on the back "I survived Allegany State Park." The Administration objected. But we sold them out any way.

Hook France and an Allegany State Park Stock Car
Courtesy of Bob Byledbal

"Our ice came from the ice house in Salamanca. It got there by railroad refrigerator car from the Adirondacks in 300 pound chunks. They'd cut them into 25-pound pieces that we sold for 25 cents. People used to complain about the price. Now 25 pounds costs $3.

"The Park took down the Red House Pavilion in 1952. The Quaker dancehall came down just a few years ago. When we had square dances, Leo Remington used to be the caller,

Rube Strickland played the violin. Rube was the music teacher over at the high school. Everybody loved the last dance of the night and you'd try to get your best gal as a partner. Leo would call:

'Okay, promenade on the outside
On the inside dos-e-dos
A-le-main right and
Swing your partner
When you meet her
Then you hug her
And you kiss her--- if you can.'"

While Bob caught his breath, someone in the audience asked, "What were the most popular items you sold?"

Bob's 45 RPM Collection
Courtesy of Bob Byledbal

Without hesitating he answered, "Beer and pop. We sold a lot of bread and milk and newspapers, too. There was Blue Boy pop. A local cannery did vegetables in the summer and to stay busy they canned pop in the winter. A 12-ounce bottle sold for 7 cents, a case was $1.60.

"People used to cut their feet on the pop tops. The Administration complained and we had to make the employees open them in the store.

"We had a fire inspector come through. He complained, 'Why do you keep that door closed. It's dangerous.' So I had the help keep it open. Then a health inspector saw it and he complained, 'You keep that door open, you're going to have flies in here.' So I told them to close it. Wound up telling them, 'If he looks like a health inspector, close it. If you think he's a fire inspector, open it up.'

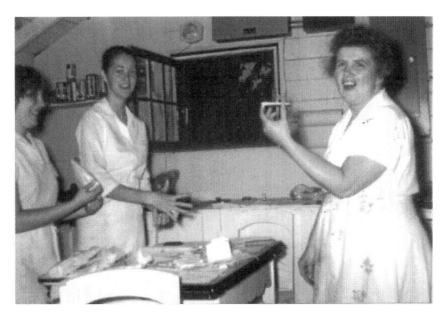

Red House Pavilion Kitchen Staff 1960
Courtesy of Bob Byledbal

A shout came from the audience, "How about bears?"

"Our employees were all good kids. They've gone off all over the world now. I get cards from everywhere. But there was the yearly Employee's Party. We let them do whatever. They trucked an outhouse painted like a toll booth to the entrance. The Administration saw it go by and just looked the other way. They painted on it 'Deposit here.' Somehow, a car always wound up in the lake.

"People would always go up to the dump in the evening to watch bears. I drove up there to get rid of our garbage. My wife was along. The mother bear was down in the gully and her two cubs came up behind me. She charged. My wife yelled and I jumped in the truck just in time. A big gang watched the show.

"We had a laundry. A lady came into the store and said, 'you gotta' see this.'

"There was a drunk in the laundry. He had taken off all his clothes and stood there naked. He said, 'My clothes got dirty. I had to wash 'em.'

"Ostrander Curve is down past Ryan Trail toward Bradford. There have been three or four fatalities there, especially when the Saddle House was running. The creek made for fog. It was a sharp turn and the curve on it is banked the wrong way. I know there are at least two people in the room today who went into that ditch.

"Ed Nagle ran the Saddle House on the Red House entrance just past the toll booth. There were motel rooms and at the bar he had horse saddles for stools. Outside there was a little amusement park with tiny cars that needed a shove to get up over the hill. He had a furnace back up and five girls were killed. He never got over that.

"In 1978 things were really getting bad. The Chosen Few motorcycle gang was bringing in prostitutes and drugs. The Administration would try to keep them out. They'd rent a cabin under some other name.

"Once, I had about $1000 to deposit in the bank. That was a lot of money then. There was a car ahead of me going twenty miles an hour. This black van conversion started to run my tail. I went up to fifty. I ducked down into the pine trees with my lights out. They passed and I called the police. About 3am those guys burned their van. They must have thought I got their plate number.

Bob Holding Forth in the Quaker Dancehall at its Last Dance
Courtesy of Bob Byledbal

"Canadians were doing a big marijuana business down here. They had a cabin on Horseshoe Trail. One of the Park cops was laying in the grass alongside the cabin to listen to their plans. He had on a new Stetson hat. Someone came out in the dark to pee off the porch and spoiled the hat.

"Over in Quaker the Chosen Few gang had 50-60 people. They had chopped up a cabin porch for a campfire. A Park cop went in and they threw him out. He called Bradford, Salamanca and all around. Forty to sixty police cars came. They surrounded the place with shotguns and ushered 200 people out of the Park.

"We had enough. It wasn't long after that we closed up shop and left."

Bob got a big round of applause but the crowd wouldn't let him go so he encored for a while. The one I caught was when someone yelled "Tell about your 'Park Wife?'"

"Oh, yeah" he said. "Charlie Lapp was one of the Park Police. He was an imposing person. I'm this little nineteen-year-old. He comes up to me and says, 'You're going to hire my wife.' I did and she ran the store for me. She was my 'park wife.' She thought she was a police officer. Once, I found a kid under a car out in front of the store. He said, 'I'm not coming out of here 'till that lady goes away.'

Glass Flying-Red-Horse Globe that stood in front of the Red House Store from 1941-50
Courtesy of Bob Byledbal

"We'd never sell white gas in a glass container. It was too dangerous. A guy tried to talk her into it once and she blew up at him. He stormed out the door and ran into Charlie in uniform. 'Officer, that lady in there swore at me.' 'You mean my wife?' Charlie said."

Bob is one of the best story tellers on our Historical Society roster. This is at least his third appearance for us. We'll probably try to get him back next year.

GEORGE HERON
ONE MORE STORY

May 2009

George Heron Camp Allegany 2009

George Heron was President of the Seneca Nation for six years during the struggle against the Kinzua Dam. He won three decorations while serving in US Navy during World War

II and he helped build Allegany State Park while a member of Roosevelt's CCC.

In his late eighties George Heron came to the Allegany State Park Historical Society's June 2009 Retreat at Camp Allegany. He has slowed a bit since he last spoke to us. Now he walks with a cane and wheels an oxygen bottle along behind him for extra breath. He rested in a chair and paused frequently as he spoke. Audience questions had to be amplified or repeated for him to hear them but the twinkle remained in his eye as he spun his stories.

Here is an approximation of what the old warrior had to say about Allegany:

"I joined the CCC in 1936 and Allegany State Park was my home for two years. It paid a dollar a day, fed you, gave you a place to sleep and drink. Genesee Ale was three for twenty-five cents. Picked up a few bad habits while I was here, too," he laughed."

Civilian Conservation Corps at Harrisville New York

"My first trip through here was in a 1926 or 27 Model T Run About. It was all open fields filled with wild strawberries. There was no lake. It was all farms through here.

"This place where we are meeting today, Camp Allegany, was Sprucelands, a woman's camp. They had horses."

George's recollection reminded me of when I was a camp counselor in 1952 at Arrowhead, Camp 12. One of my jobs was to take the kids to Sprucelands where we had a pleasant break from routine, riding horses.

"My CCC outfit built the Ryan Trail cabins and Beehunter and Congdon. Lot of them are torn down now.

"Over to Bay State we cut down all the dead chestnut trees killed by the blight. We skidded them out, used them for guard rails along the lake. They are gone now.

"Six years ago at our CCC reunion we planted some immune chestnut trees. I've never been back to check whether they grew."

At this point Jim Carr came in with plastic tubing around his neck and trailing an oxygen bottle just like George's. George interrupted to wave hello and chuckling said, "We belong to the same club." Jim smiled and waved back.

George went on, "Down around Camp Turner there is one living chestnut tree that survived the blight."

George's mention of that 2002 reunion reminded me that I was there and had six or seven CCCs and some of their wives telling stories into a tape recorder. I hope that tape is still somewhere in the Park archives.

"The CCC built roads in the Park. We built the one up over the hill from Salamanca. Before that we used to use that road down below the dam.

"The last CCC camp left here in 1942. Everyone was going to the Army or the Navy.

"At our last reunion here in the Park there were only five of us left so we discontinued them.

Seventh Annual
CIVILIAN CONSERVATION CORPS REUNION

ALLEGANY STATE PARK
May 14, 1997

Commemorating Historic Preservation Week

STATE OF NEW YORK
Office of Parks, Recreation and Historic Preservation
George E. Pataki, Governor
Bernadette Castro, Commissioner
Edward Rutkowski, District Director
WESTERN DISTRICT - ALLEGANY REGION

Civilian Conservation Corps

1933-1942

"The Boys That Made Roosevelt Famous"

"The CCC was the best thing that ever happened to us. During the Depression, there were food lines, no jobs. Amish brought produce they couldn't sell into town and gave it away.

Depression days were not as bad in the country as in the city. You could grow your own food in the country.

"The first CCC camp was in tents on the Scenic Highway. Then there was one on the Bradford Road. Then they built a barracks by the ski run. World War I vets had their own camp. All the colored CCCs were over in Hungry Hollow. They didn't stay long. People in Salamanca didn't want them in their theater. There were Brooklyn CCCs. They didn't speak the same language."

George tried his Brooklyn accent on us, 'Toity-toid Street.' And there was the Alabama group. They'd say, 'You all and ah reckin.' There was a number of CCCs from Jamestown and Olean. Once there were eight hundred of us in the Park alone, not counting vets.

"There's only one building left, the Infirmary.

"We ate pretty well. We weren't bona fide cooks. Didn't have to be. If the platters were empty they'd eat that.

All these CCC recollections of George's took me back to the late thirties when I was a camper at Camp 12. It was then the old German Buffalo Turnverein Camp. I have absolutely no recollection of the CCC presence in the Park then. What I do recall was visiting with my family, my uncle Bernard in a CCC Camp on the edge of the Adirondacks. And I remember how helpful his government pay was to my struggling grandmother and grandfather.

Bob Schmid then asked George, "As a Native American in the Park, did you ever run into any discrimination?"

George cupped his ear, "Didn't hear that." Bob shouted his question back.

George answered an emphatic "No." Then added "There were six of us Bucks from one barracks. We all worked together."

He went on, "I helped cut down the poplars. Sent them to the paper mill in Red House. "Clarence Watt and one of the

Jimersons hand-hewed all those timbers in the Red House Administration Building.

Red House Administration Building

Red House Administration Building Beamed Ceiling

"I attended the grand opening of the Red House Dam. There was a large number of people there. The Red House Administration Building was already open and operating. The Allegany State Park marching band played for the opening.

"Floyd Printup, a relative of mine, played the alto horn in the band. They had one trombone. I'd come to listen to them rehearse. Half were Park employees. Old man Carr, Howard Carr, played the bass drum. Had his grandson Jim carry it for him when they were in a parade. He didn't want to quit.

"When the Park opened full blast, jobs opened up. There were mostly Anglo Saxons living in Red House except for one Italian family. The Fanchers, the Carrs and the Frances controlled the jobs. They passed them down to the next generation, father to son. The Park plumber, the Master Engineer passed the job father to son.

George paused for a moment; looked up at the ceiling tapped his cane as if trying to capture another thought along that line. He looked back at us saying "Memory fades."

Then he smiled and said, "Ed Nagel set up business at the Red House entrance to the Park, the Saddle House Restaurant. He had different kinds of rides, a railroad, Lil Toot."

"I've been into the hills, too, for a bit of larceny. My wife drops me off over in Bay State to look for ginseng. There is a lot of money in it now. Used to be only twelve dollar a pound. What does it look like? It has three branches, all come out of one spot and a red flower in August. Root shape of a human with arms and legs. Supposed to be an aphrodisiac. That's why there are so many Chinamen," he chuckled.

Bob Schmid asked, "What about Witch's Walk?"

George responded "The Gahine, that mysterious light, strange things happen there, the ghost of John Lawson, the giant who's buried by his cabin in there. There was a fella' over in Cold Spring. His aunt wanted some princess pine herb. He went looking for it in there. It was dusk, getting dark. Something was approaching him along the railroad track. Looked like a giant. He felt a warmth and ah-ah presence. The fella ran, jumped in his Johnboat to get back across the river.

He walked in the house. His mother looked at him, 'Your hair's gone gray.'

"Other things happen there, too. There was a murder there. Stay away in the moonlight if you're walking by yourself.

They no longer see strange animals with the Ga-hi-ne. But they say the light is the glow of buried gold. Pete Jackson's grandfather met some deserting Union Soldiers during the Civil War. He helped them with some clothes and directions to Canada. The reward was a handful of gold. He buried it back in there and died before he could dig it up. Down at the store whenever they saw his grandson walking by, they'd call 'There goes Pete looking for gold.'

This story of George's was familiar to me. I heard him tell a more elaborate version along with some others ten years ago. I've got them recorded in my book which I freely advertise here, *"Allegany Hellbender Tales."*

The Last Allegany State Park CCC Reunion
George Heron at right

George paused again, looked around, sighed quietly and said, "I guess I've overstayed my leave."

The group chorused back "Oh no, keep going." Bob asked, "What about the Black School?"

George said, "That was the Darcy home. Mrs. Darcy was a nurse. She took care of eight or ten little black children. It closed when she passed."

George shrugged. "I'm running out of steam. If I felt better I'd talk longer."

This time, we let him go. We gave him a warm round of applause and we all moved over to the mess hall for a grand spaghetti dinner followed by a campfire with more stories, a few songs and a lot of conversation.

LYN'S FIRST TRIPS TO ALLEGANY STATE PARK

Lyn Beahan, May 2010

While Larry's first recollections of The Park date from 1934, my first trip to Allegany was in 1950 when some Alpha Gam sorority friends stayed part of our UB winter break at the Parallel Trail cabin of one of our classmates, Dolores Bogulski Kuberka. It seemed like the coldest January on record and we spent most of the time playing Canasta and cooking and eating. We must have ventured out though because I found this picture at the old Fancher Pool in Quaker Run with Peg Malley, Norma Enquist, Me, Nan Dossert and Bebe Crone.

Winter Break, Fancher Pool 1950

My next trip was when I got my first car in '53 just before we were married and Larry suggested a drive to the Park.

My '51 Chevy Club Coupe Red House 1953

Later that summer we worked as counselors at Camp Arrowhead (Camp 12).

"Happy Birthday Larry" Aug 10 1953

RICK FEUZ AND HIS VOLUNTEERS

January 2010

Rick Feuz January, 2010

Rick Feuz has been Program Chair for the Allegany State Park Historical Society for the past few years. He has scouted out speaker after speaker to describe their experiences in the Park and in that way painted a portrait of Allegany's history for us. At the same time, he was, in fact, painting the Park. He and his crew of high school kids were painting the cabins and guard rails of the Park "Allegany Green." In

January of this year he scheduled himself as our speaker and came forward with an account of that volunteer work.

It was a snowy winter day. The historical Society met indoors in the Administration Building's museum. The great room was being re-plastered. Rick had the museum ready for his slide show. He, himself, was dressed as usual in dungarees and boots but had a hooded sweat shirt pulled on over his work shirt.

National Public Lands Day, Sept 29
Volunteers come together to perform service projects on public Lands across the United States

He teaches English at the Cattaraugus High School though he comes across more like their football coach. He began "I was born in Fort Monroe Virginia but raised in Buffalo. Our first vacation was a trip to Allegany State Park.

My Dad loved Dowd Trail so we always went there. Growing up, I remember the dances. When I graduated from college there was a job open in Cattaraugus. I grabbed it and have been in and around the Park ever since.

"In 2005 I did some work in the Park as a volunteer with National Public Lands Day and I joined the Historical Society. Up till then I had imagined there was a crew of workmen in the Park at dawn every day taking care of the place. I found that wasn't so and there was a lot of work that wasn't getting done.

Paint Crew from Cattaraugus High School
Courtesy of Rick Feuz

"Our school requires 20 hours of public service in order to graduate. There is not enough work in the town to go around for all the students. So I decided to bring these healthy 17-18 year old kids down here to help out. I've got this great big long volunteer form that the kids' parents have to sign, giving permission."

As Rick talked he clicked a remote that flashed on the screen photos of his crews at work or posing or goofing around. They looked dirty and sweaty but happy.

Trail Crew from Cattaraugus High
Courtesy of Rick Feuz

"Our first trip was to work on the trails in the Hurricane Blow-down Site on ASP1. And there I met Tim O'Keefe. He met us, showed us what had to be done and since then he has become my best friend. . Whenever our crews need anything he arranges it.

"He is devoted to the Park. I've seen him cleaning up broken beer bottles in the men's John and his attitude is, 'The customer is always right.' He is a single guy and runs the cleaning staff which is all women. When they work, there is an incredible amount of estrogen in the air.

"Tim comes from Niagara Falls. As a kid when his family was in the Park he'd be walking along the roads picking up garbage. He loved the Park so much he moved to Salamanca and agreed to take any job they offered. He wound up cleaning toilets. You'd see him riding his bike to work up the Scenic Hi-way from Salamanca.

Rick Demonstrating Two-man Cross-cut Saw
Courtesy of Rick Feuz

"We've done a lot of trail work. We've done Osgood Trail three times. It is the trail from hell. It is so steep. We've done Black Snake three times, Bear Caves twice, Eastwood Meadows and the Bear Spring Ring. It just takes muscle and time.

"From April till the tourists come is our busiest. Other teachers go to Florida. I come and play in the woods. One of the kids was talking to a Park worker and I heard him say,

'You mean you get paid to work in the woods? How do I get hired?'

"I have a few rules. I won't take any work that belongs to any Park employee. As far as the kids go, no alcohol or drugs, no offensive politics or religion. There's never any fighting. I wouldn't put up with it. I'm the mean guy. Everyone wears boots and gloves. One kid brought a machete. I put it in the trunk of the car. I have bandages, toilet paper and cell phone in a pack. No one has ever been cut, so far. One time a tree with a big butt attached shifted and hoisted up one of the guys between the legs. They all got a big laugh.

**Before Painting
Courtesy of Rick Feuz**

"When we work on cabins we paint and pull staples. I've got this contractor friend, Rich. He's a real angry guy on the phone. But with all the pollution regulations, it costs him more to 'hazmat' leftover paint than to give it to me, even though he has to get it shaded Allegany Green.

"We've painted the cabins on Ryan Trail." Here Rick showed before-painting and after-painting shots of the cabins on Ryan trail. A crew stood proudly in front of a finished job. "Over at France Brook we painted Camp 12, at one cabin per hour. We did the insides white. They made the bunks so you can't get them out the door to steal them. We had to paint around them, move them and paint again. There is a grant in the mill to pay for repairing the cabins on Beehunter. We may get help from Teachers Center Inc. and from Habitat for Humanity.

After Painting
Courtesy of Rick Feuz

"Up at the end of Red House Lake, the main building at Camp Allegany had to be re-stained. Here is a picture before and after."

I think one of those was where he showed a kid painting in stocking feet. Rick explained, "He showed up in these $150 sneakers. His father is an old student of mine. He'd have screamed.

"While we were there this beautiful young girl in shorts came over and asked what we were doing. I told her and she asked if she could help. She pitched right in. I told the guys later this was why they needed a higher education.

"We worked on Wayne Robins' sugar shanty at Camp Allegany. He has this 300-pound iron kettle that he always has trouble getting up on the hill for the maple sugar demonstration. The kids carried it up when we weren't looking. It's dangerous. They might have dropped it on one of them.

"I'm a teacher from the old school. I'm not the pat-'em-on-the-head type. I'm more 'Get it done or I'll kill you.' I spread them out about twenty feet apart to keep them from talking too much. Most of the kids are football players and they are amazingly strong. We use axes and two-man cross-cut saws and carry them in to the job. But somehow I'm always the one who winds up carrying the 32-pound pry bar. We never use chain saws. There's a 12-hour training course required before you can use one in the Park."

Rick stopped at one of the pictures and said, "This one is a State Trooper, and this one plays college football out west. Joe is a diabetic. He gives himself insulin shots when he takes a break from sawing.

He stopped again at a picture of the guard rail on the highway around Red House Lake. It was painted a nice bright green. "We had flagmen out there and everything," he said. "We got this about half done. Then someone came by from the office. 'Better hold up. The Administration is not sure they like the color,' she said.

"'Go tell, 'em, 'it's All American John Deere Green.' That seemed to take care of it. We had to come back seven times to finish up and I was thrilled when it was done.

"This is the Bear Spring Trail. There's a bog across it about a quarter mile in," he said as a picture appeared on the screen with four grinning teen-agers standing by a pile of woodchips five feet high. "It took seventy-two wheelbarrow trips to carry those wood chips in." Then he showed us another picture with the four, still smiling but sweat-soaked and the pile, gone."

This story of Rick's must go to the heart of what has made the human species so successful. To take a bunch of healthy young folks out in the woods, repair a cabin or fix a trail, laughing, sweating and getting something done, sounds to me like one of the best good times that can be had. And in tonight's Buffalo News I read that the NY State Parks budget may be cut back by 40%.

Thanks Rick for helping to keep Allegany in shape.

MERCY KILLED TOOTS

June 2009

We were sitting around a bonfire at Camp Allegany. The sky was black. Only one star had come out but it was cold enough that the black flies had gone in.

Mercy Holiday at Breakfast Camp Allegany 2009

The singing faded out after "I Been Workin' on the Railroad" We fell into small conversation groups or just sat staring into the flames.

I sat next to a cheerful lady, a couple years more ancient than myself, Mercy Holiday by name. She has worked in the Park her whole life. At dinner in the mess hall I overheard her say quietly, "I won't be back to work this summer…some health issues."

We'd never talked much so out at the fire, I idly asked, "Where are you from?" Turned out she and I were both born on Northampton on Buffalo's old German East Side. That launched her on the story of how she killed Toots, her Aunt Kate's pet turtle.

"My dad," she said, "loved turtle soup. Every year his brother would bring a big snapper home from Canada. They'd kill it and make soup. The head would stay alive a long time and hang on to a stick with his beak. We kids would go waving it around.

"Aunt Kate had a pet turtle, a painted turtle. Dad always teased he'd make soup out of it. She got it when it was real small and kept it for seventy-five years.

"He would come when she called, 'Here Toots.' He would go out on the porch and set in the sun when she told him, 'go on out there.' She had a little stand she'd put him on and tell him 'just look out the window,' and he would stay right there staring.

"All she ever fed him was lettuce and water. He was very well-mannered, never messed. Well, maybe he'd leave a little wet spot. Always did his duty in the water. She had a baby bathtub for him to swim around in. He slept on a pillow under her big claw-legged bath tub. Slept from October to May. She'd tell him to go to bed and he'd go in there.

"Once she asked me to get his nails cut. I called the Vet and asked 'Could you cut the toe nails on my aunt's pet turtle?' He said, 'Sure thing; bring him over.' When I got there, he laughed, 'I thought you were kidding,' but he went ahead and trimmed them. He examined Toots, too. Found out he was a girl. I told Aunt Kate but she was always convinced he was a boy.

"She was a big woman with a big chest. She'd sit rocking in her chair with him on her chest and talk to him. That turtle traveled all over the world, even on airplanes. She carried him in this little bag. They must have thought it was her clothes.

"In her nineties she went to a nursing home. They wouldn't let him go along. So I had to take him. She had been to the zoo and seen alligators in with the turtles and was afraid he'd get eaten. I wound up with Toots and I killed him. I didn't have the time to talk to him or rock him like she did and he died of a broken heart.

He woke up one day. Took a few steps off his pillow, didn't see Aunt Kate and he fell over dead. My husband took him up on the hill to bury him. I wish I'd of thought to ask him where. I'd 've dug up his shell and kept it for a souvenir."

GRACE CHRISTY
AND THE
CCC

May 2009

Grace Christy has been an Allegany State Park Naturalist for many years. She had the opportunity in that time to accumulate a treasure trove of Allegany lore. The Park Administration, recognizing that, recently made her Park Archivist. She agreed to share with us her knowledge of the Civilian Conservation Corps in Allegany. This session of the Historical Society convened in the Red House Administration Building's museum where Grace could illustrate her talk using the audio visual equipment she has managed for many years.

Unfortunately Grace's slides were not available for this book so I will do my best with descriptions of them and pictures from my own collection. Fortunately my uncle, Bernard Beahan, was a member of a CCC unit at Harrisville, NY on the edge of the Adirondacks. I visited him there in 1937 and have included a few of his pictures to illustrate life in the CCC.

CCC Member on Garbage Detail

Grace began, "The Park has tons of stuff in its archives. What I have today is a slide show I put together for one of the Allegany State Park Civilian Conservation Corps' reunions.

The CCC was Roosevelt's "Tree Army." FDR (President Franklin Delano Roosevelt) was Governor of New York State till 1931, President of the United States from '32 till he died just before the end of WWII in 1945. In the 30's, the middle of the Depression, he started the CCC. He gave them one main duty: to plant trees all over the country.

"We are in another economic slump but somehow now we don't seem to be able to work together like we did back then. The Parks cooperated with the Army and provided places for the CCC camps to be set up. The Department of Agriculture, working under the Department of the Interior, laid out and supervised the work the CCC was to do. We put hundreds of thousands of young men to useful work, paid them, reforested the country and got some beautiful work done in the Parks.

Stone Tower built by the CCC at the Summitt

"We don't seem able to cooperate like that anymore."
Grace's first slide was an old map of Allegany State Park illustrating the locations of several of its CCC camps. She

pointed to a spot on the map, "This is where Company 249 was located, SP (State Park Camp) 33. It was the first CCC camp on the Red House side of the Park. Company 249 started the work on the Stone Tower which is located at the Summit near the Art Roscoe Ski Area. "If you stand on the tower and look just below, that's where their tents were."

She showed us pictures of the tower itself, views from it, the stone arrow designed into its deck and some of the now-deteriorating masonry inside. Grace commented, "You used to get beautiful views of the stars up there. Now they are blocked by trees and there is too much light from Salamanca. The Casino finally killed it."

I recalled a photo of my wife, Lyn, and me taken up on the tower during our honeymoon working in the Park the summer of 1953 and another of us there just about 50 years later. We were skinnier on the first one; the foliage was leaner, too.

Then Grace flashed a picture of SP 33, a collection of pyramid-shaped WWI surplus tents. "Looks like an Indian village," she commented. "They were there from June till November 1933."

The next slide showed men in 30's-style felt hats and cloth caps working on a road. "Here is an antique tractor," she said. "These men were building a new road to the Summit. Some of you will remember that there used to be an entrance to the Park from the middle of Salamanca up passed the Stone Tower. It would be fun to locate these photos with a GPS".

"The first camp in the Park, one day ahead of SP 33, was Company 1288 at SP Camp 27. They were located on Park Highway 2 beyond France Brook in Quaker Run. Their actual Post Office was Bradford because they were listed by whatever was closest. There is a story about them having to move from camp to camp in Quaker in the middle of a snowstorm."

Grace showed another old Park map. "Notice there is no road up to Thunder Rock. Company 1288 built the Ridge Road to get you there." Next was another crew building that road. It showed tree stumps cut off four or five-foot high. "Here they are cutting trees and digging stumps. It's been said that a lot of naughty words were left buried there under that road. You see how they left the stumps tall to allow leverage for working them out, an awful job. They used a lot of dynamite, too, to make gravel. They wore no protective gear. OSHA would have had a nightmare."

Next was a picture of a wooden ladder to a platform on top of one of the Thunder Rocks. I remember climbing that in 1953 and being disappointed when I returned in the 80's to find it gone. OSHA must have had a nightmare about that, too.

Grace said, "SP Camp18 built the ladder.

"Here's a slide of Camp 18's tree nursery," she said, showing us bare-chested young guys standing among rows of pine saplings. "The CCC put in all these pine plantations in the Park. They were not so careful then about using native species or about diversity. We are very careful about that now.

Grace at Thunder Rock

"Do you remember the lagoon at the Quaker picnic area?" Grace asked, "It disappeared about the time I started work here." She showed a picture of the stone work being constructed by CCC boys.

Next slide was a very attractive stone bridge of which there are a few in the Park. "This was not built by the CCC. A very common mistake," she said, "is to assume that all the stone work in the Park was done by the CCC."

"They did build the zoo behind the Administration Building and the picnic shelters." Grace showed us slides of these.

"At Twin Springs near Science Lake they built this 65,000-gallon underground tank out of steel-reinforced-concrete." It acted as a reservoir to supply water to Quaker up until 1980." She showed us a picture of a couple sweating young guys pushing a wheelbarrow full of concrete. "This is the sort of infrastructure which they were responsible for that doesn't show: waterlines, sewers, buried electric cables. A lot of it is still in use today.

Bridge on ASP I

"Here is a shot of the Quaker Amphitheater site," she said. "It was taken after the snowstorm of February 1936. They made use of the natural slope and made benches of chestnut logs. The blight killed the chestnuts so they were logged off. Here is a shot of it in 1978 when I came here. We had shows three nights a week, comedy, nature, Disney and I spent many a night on that cement block in the middle there, working the projector.

"The CCC built the ski-jumps off the hill behind the Administration Building," she said, as she showed several shots of intrepid ski-jumpers in the air and one on the ground. As that one appeared she narrated in sports-commentator style, "And they fall…quite a spill." She had shots from the first day of jumping in the 30's and the last, in February 1979.

Zoo Foundation and Interpretive Kiosk, 2010

She had a photo of Company 249 at SP Camp19, a formation of men in uniform standing inspection, and then a shot of their field kitchen. Those pictures brought to my mind the summer of, I think it was 1936, when my dad took us to visit his younger brother, Bernard, who was in a CCC camp in Harrisville on the edge of the Adirondacks. I watched Uncle Bernard in a race where teams of about six men locked legs around each other in a line. And then using their hands as feet, they raced like giant caterpillars. It looked like a lot of fun, like summer camp and Gramma and Grampa were very happy to get those government checks my uncle earned.

Grace illustrated with a photo of another barracks as she spoke, "WW1 Veterans, older men, used this camp on ASP 3 in Quaker Run. Later the Diocese of Buffalo bought it and made it into Camp Turner. Camp Turner was re-built across the road from that site a few years ago."

CCC Red House Log Cabin

"I had an argument with a Park worker once. She insisted that her father had, as a member of the CCC, hewn beams for the Red House Administration Building. The Administration Building went up in the late 20's before there was any CCC. But they did build the Quaker Rental Office which also has hewn beams. That's where her father must have done his work."

The CCC, in their road and cabin building, cut down some trees as well as planting them. We saw views of them skidding logs in winter with a tractor and of the works inside the sawmill with its WW1 steam boiler and great shiny circular saw blades. We saw a WW1 surplus Thompson truck, horses and a steam shovel in use building roads and we saw cabins under construction.

"The CCC built the Ryan and Kaiser Trail cabins. The Kaiser cabins had fireplaces. Number Three burned recently. Some hunters went away and left the fire untended. The CCC built Anderson and Macintosh Trails and this lean-to. They built the Bova ski area." Grace showed the lean-to and then kids riding the rope tow at Bova.

CCC Cooks at Harrisville, NY, 1937
Uncle Bernard Beahan second from left

Listening to Grace, I was reminded of eating lunch at that North Country Trail lean-to, skiing Bova in the early 50's and how much my dad loved the new cabins on Ryan trail with their fireplaces.

Grace tossed in that she had spoken to Irving Nablock who had written for the SP Camp 51 Newsletter which they called, "Nature Notes."

As it happens, during his tour in the CCC my uncle, Bernard Beahan, wrote humor for "Outlook," the Harrisville Camp Newsletter. In his column he supported Roosevelt and the Democrats with this jibe at one of his CCC buddies, "Vandewater, our Staunch Republican, is becoming known as the-dog-that-bit-the-hand-that-fed him, wise up Vande."

Grace showed shots of the Red House picnic shelters and restrooms under construction in the 30's and of the stone pier being repaired when they lowered Red House Lake in 2001. "These are just some of the things the CCC did in the Park," she said, "the National Archives has a notebook that lists all of their projects and who worked on each of them.

"In 1937 the economy was recovering, jobs were more available and the CCC left the Park. It had been a blessing for the Park and for the men. They were paid a dollar a day. They kept $5 and the government sent $25 home to their families. There was an educational component, too. Many of them learned to read and write in the CCC.

Allegany State Park would never have been the same without them. Thank you, you CCC guys."

JOAN MILLIGAN ALLEGANY COMMISSIONER

November 2005

I was wary when I called Joan Milligan with an invitation to speak to the Allegany Historical Society at Red House. She had been a member of the Allegany State Park Commission for thirty years and spent the last several of those presiding at Red House as Chair of the Commission. On many occasions during her tenure, I had spoken out in print opposing lumbering and gas and development in the Park, policies I believed she cherished. So my phone call to invite her to Red House felt like TV's Jon Stewart inviting President George Bush to the White House.

Our mutual friend, Bob Schmid, tried to reassure me, I thought overeagerly, "Oh, she likes you. At least you spend time in the Park. She knows you love the Park." I was unsettled. But when I called, the Commissioner was cordial and agreed.

On the appointed day, the Red House Administration Building awaited at its prime, commanding the shimmering lake that reflected a blue October sky on a couch of hills draped in red, green and yellow. I met Andy Malicki, our Society president, in the lobby in front of the paneled and many-windowed great room where we expected to meet. "We've got a glich. There's a wedding in the great room."

In the summer the Historical Society meets in St. John's-in-the-Woods on the Quaker side of the Park; during the rest of the year we meet at Red House. This was to be our first fall meeting and we had neglected to notify anyone that we were coming back. It looked like Commissioner Milligan would have to deliver her address in the confined space of the Administration Building Museum. This seemed an affront and we used that as leverage in a number of hurried contacts. The police dispatcher got the Officer-in-Charge on the phone. That officer hurried in from his patrol, assessed the situation and called Park Supervisor, Mike Miecznikowski. Mike said that since the second floor Administration Building restaurant was not in use we could meet there if we could locate the concessionaire-operator and get permission. The Administration Building front desk had the telephone number of the concessionaire, the Double Diamond Grill in Salamanca. The Officer called the grill and fortunately the owner was tending bar in a good mood and gave us the OK. This took about an hour. Then as we were opening the restaurant doors and cranking up its ancient steam radiators to take the chill off the spacious room the Commissioner and her husband, Dan Milligan, arrived.

Commissioner Joan Milligan 2005

I think I should call her Joan from here on since she and Dan turned out to be pretty informal, easy-to-get-along-with people, and in-person we were on a first name basis. Let me qualify that. The Milligans lived near JN Adam Memorial Hospital at Perrysburg and recently I had been involved in trying to keep 450 acres of forest there from being sold to a lumbering outfit. I started to touch on that hoping for support but Joan's hackles went up. She stated briefly and firmly her position favoring timber harvesting. I mounted a similar brief defense of forest preservation. Then we took a breath and quickly arrived at a truce in which we agreed that some amount of primitive forest should be preserved for bio-diversity and pleasure and another lumbered for the wood products the world needs, each reserving our own idea of what the proportions should be. Then we changed the subject and got along just fine.

Dan and Joan Milligan

I introduced Joan to the crowd of old timers, most of whom she had known longer than I had. I told them Joan was a Registered Nurse. She had worked at Buffalo General and later as a Community Mental Health Nurse in Gowanda. She had been an Allegany State Park Commissioner for 30 years and in 1985 became Chair of the Commission.

Joan is in her vigorous upper-middle years. She wears glasses and was dressed in a blue turtle, jeans and a navy blue blazer, with an American flag pin in the lapel. I will try to give you the gist of her recollections:

"Thirty years ago on a gorgeous day at the peak of the season, a day about like this, I went to my first Commissioners meeting. It was a joint meeting with other regions and it was at Letchworth Park. As a kid my family went to Letchworth a lot and I had an emotional attachment to the place. That first meeting of mine was in 1970.

"I was not the first woman Commissioner. Katie Hall was first. Mr. Carr remembers her." Former Park Administration officer, Jim Carr, sitting nearby nodded and chuckled his assent.

"The Parks were under the DEC (Department of Environmental Conservation) until 1960. Then the Parks and Recreation Law placed them under OPRHP (Office of Parks Recreation and Historic Preservation.). Article 7 provided for twelve Park Regions and for seven Commissioners in this Western Region that includes Allegany State Park. We were to meet four times a year and review the budget and the Park Administration's application of State policy. We were to give our advice and represent the citizen's viewpoint while maintaining close liaison with the Park supervisory people.

"We had seven-year terms. There was a gentleman's agreement that Allegany and Erie County would get one Commissioner each, Chautauqua two and Cattaraugus three. I was first appointed by Governor Hugh Carey and twice by Cuomo. I served under three Regional Directors, Ron Bach, Hugh Dunn and Jim Rich. In 1985 I became Chair of the Commission and began going to State Council of Parks meetings. Bill Taylor was chair before me and Dalton Burget after. I served under three OPRHP Commissioners.

"There were many highlights to my time here. The bike path around Red House Lake was for families. It got a lot of users. The Quaker Store Museum was a great success and it was very appropriate that it was dedicated to Senator Jess Present while he was still alive. He brought so much money to the Park.

Quaker Store Museum at Park's 75th Birthday Party 1996

"We had one meeting of the New York Council of Parks here that gave us the chance to showcase Allegany. But my fondest memories are of the 75th birthday we gave Allegany in 1996.

"One of my worst memories is of Allegany-green paint. Albany said 'green.' We wanted brown and finally, after many years, they let us have brown on the Fancher Cottages in Quaker.

"One of the best things about the job was all of the extra time I got to spend in the Park.

"The disappearance of Fancher Pool was a big disappointment. Our cabin was right across from it. I loved it, my family loved it, the campers loved it but, the people up above called the shots and it went.

"Another disappointment was a lodge. Many parks have lodges, not motels but really comfortable places to stay. The Summit near the cross-country ski trails would have been an ideal site.

Fancher Cabin

"Each Commissioner gets a cabin. I was given the old Fancher Cabin with an indoor toilet. The traditional Allegany cabins with nothing but a wood stove and no indoor plumbing were OK 50 years ago, but they weren't really fun for a mom who works out of the house. OPRHP Commissioner Bernadette Castro came here, looked at the situation and pushed it for us. We compromised on the new Fancher Trail Cottages where they even supply linen.

"I always thought that we should have made a major Park entrance off Route 219 at Limestone. That would have opened up the Park to that whole area. We had considered making a third major section to the Park that would be accessed from Limestone."

Joan concluded, "It has been a privilege and honor to serve the southern tier. I did not always agree with all of my constituents but I tried to present the view of the majority, not just that of the vocal minority."

With that we all gave Joan a round of applause and when it subsided she agreed to answer questions.

Bernie Sheffer had asked one about land donated to the Park which Joan could not answer though she knew of many land donations.

A woman in the audience said, "We were one of the first to stay in the Fancher Cottages. Someone came by and asked if they could bring some State people in to look. Fifteen of them marched through."

Bob Schmid asked, "How come most of the Park money goes south to Taconic Park and down that way?"

Joan answered, "The money is allotted according to Park attendance. In the old days when we had the dancehalls and that sort of thing, Allegany had a lot heavier attendance. And of course New York City has half the state population."

Rose Marie Budnick piped up, "But aren't our cabins filled most of the time?"

Joan replied. "At one time, not one penny of cabin rental money stayed in the Park. Now most of it does and so do some of the gate fees."

As the questions wound down, I thought better of raising the idea that some of us really liked the old cabins with their wood stoves, or that half the Park users come from Erie County and therefore maybe Cattaraugus's heavy representation on the Commission was out of proportion and I certainly was not going to ask about the 20-year-old Master Plan that might have scheduled regular logging in the Park except for the "vocal minority" that turned into a majority and shouted it down. So I saved those for now, and tossed a softball. I asked if she had any animal stories.

Joan concluded with a rousing round of her family's encounters with colonizing raccoons, chewing porcupines and very entertaining bears.

PART TWO

PASSIONS

BLACK BEARS
RICK ROTH

June 2010

Rick Roth and two Black Bear Skulls

Rick Roth is a very big man. Well over six foot and pushing 300 pounds. He, like another big guy, our own Bob Schmid, is fascinated by black bears. You wonder if their own hugeness makes for this fascination. But then everyone in the room at St. John's-in-the-Woods Chapel on Saturday June 19 seemed to be in love with bears.

Few could compete with Rick in the quantity of artifacts, lore, information and experience that his research has brought him. His day job is the management of a home for developmentally-disabled men. His relief from this difficult work is complete escape into the woods in search of Black Bears. At the start of his talk he stood at the podium demonstrating two black bear skulls with articulated jaws and large canines. The male skull was much larger than the female. He grinned and worked the jaws as I photographed him.

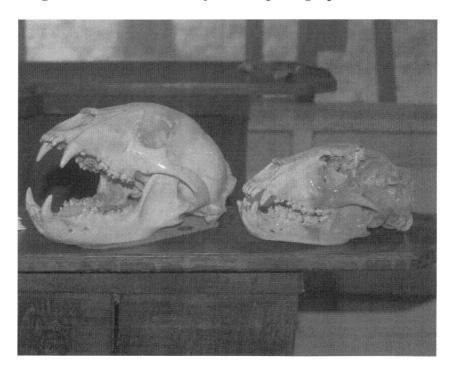

Black Bear Skulls in Profile

Rick began, "May, June, July and August, bears are mating. They are very active and it is your best chance to see them. A lot of my research is into the reaction of people to bears. When you are hiking you should get to know the area. Look for stumps that have been broken up where a bear is looking for bugs to eat. They have long sticky tongues that pick up bugs. Look for trees with the bark clawed open. Bears eat the layer between the bark and the wood of the tree.

"Look up when you are looking for bears. I stopped in a highway rest area and walked toward the back fence. I looked up at a tree. It was an amazing sight. There was this great big bear 60 to 80 feet up lying on a branch with his paws hanging down.

"Look for bear scat. I've got pictures of all kinds of bear scat. The people at work think I'm crazy for all my pictures of poop. But you can tell a lot about bears by knowing what they eat. Out at Yellowstone the Rangers tell folks to talk and make noise when they are on the trail. They urge them to wear these little bells and carry pepper spray. At the end of the lecture some tourist always asks, 'How do you tell Grizzly scat from Black Bear scat?' The Ranger explains, 'Black bear scat usually has mostly berries. Grizzly scat is full of little bells and smells peppery.'"

Rick passed his photo albums of scat to the front row to hand through the audience. "There is a picture in there of an anal mucus plug I found. It comes out at the end of hibernating. Looks just like a role of chocolate donuts." he grinned.

That album was followed by another of bear photos all taken in the wild and close up. Rick Feuz, always the well-prepared classroom teacher, began passing out the first of seven Xerox's of DEC bear information and newspaper pieces on bears.

Rick Roth went on, "Bear attacks in New York State are rare and are caused by human error. Give bears their space and they will leave you alone. I get within 20 to 30 feet, use my little digital camera with its 15 X zoom, snap one picture and back away. One picture is enough.

"I've only had a bear follow me out one time. I got in my truck. He nosed around and left.

"I live near Dansville, not far from Rattle Snake Hill. It's good bear country. When I go out looking for bears, I bring a $10.00 'Bear Bomb' to bring them in. Smells like delicious hickory smoked bacon but has no food value, so it's legal. The NY DEC has given me permission to carry pepper spray. The law is pretty strict on that. I wear a fanny pack, rather than a big back pack. I can move easier and I carry a heavy, metal walking stick. Bears are all about eating. That's all they do all the time and they use their very sensitive noses to find food. If a bear comes after you smack him on the nose.

"Some people will throw their packs at bears. That is the dumbest thing you can do. It is like feeding the bear. People bring dogs and think the dogs will protect them. They are no protection. A dog'll just aggravate a bear and bring the bear right back to you. Bears are so strong; just one swipe of a paw will take a dog out.

"Myself, I'm not a bear hunter. I've helped the DEC by showing people that hunting the only way to keep the bear population under control. Bears are prolific. A sow has three cubs every year. She will lose one, eaten by a male, but the other two survive. Some people oppose hunting but there are 6-7000 bears in New York State even though hunting takes 14-1500 of them each year. In New Jersey the Animal Rights people persuaded the legislature to ban bear hunting. Pretty soon there were so many bears in everybody's back yard and so many pets were getting eaten that they came begging for a bear hunt.

Rick referred to some of the bear pictures in the photo album which he had circulated. "That one made me sick. Some puffed up hunter shot that little bear. She was a momma with two cubs. They had been in a den. You could tell by the way her coat was matted on one side." Referring to another photo, "I found this one on Route 390 near Cohocton, a two-year-old hit by a truck." Then finally, "I took this one in Allegany State Park, a mother with five cubs. There is so much food in the Park that they can have very big litters.

Rick held up one of the DEC information sheets with a map showing the location of bear populations in New York State. He pointed to the Adirondacks, "The Adirondacks has the largest number of bears in the State. In 2002 I went up there. Camped for a week in a tent. Didn't see a thing. So we took this scenic railroad ride and there just off the right-of-way was this beautiful 500-pound gold-muzzled black bear with one gold paw.

Black Bear Up-close

Rick stopped for a moment, looked around and said, "You better ask me some questions. It works better that way."

Jerry asked, "What should you do when you meet a bear in the woods?"

Rick answered quickly, "Don't get into a situation you can't get out of, wear bells, go in a group and talk a lot. I do everything I shouldn't. I know. I'm there alone and quiet but I've got pepper spray and a big heavy walking stick.

"If you surprise a bear, back away looking at it. Make yourself look big, open up your jacket, stand on a stump, and get close to other people. Do not turn and run. That is the bear's signal to run after you and chase you down.

Rick held up for our inspection a vicious-looking black bear claw. Then he held up another shorter, broader and curved rather than straight. He said, "Bear claws interdigitate. A bear can open a jar of peanut butter."

Black Bear at the old Bova Garbage Dump
Courtesy of Bob Schmid

Ellen Gibson spoke up from the audience. "Bears must have a terrible problem with tooth decay when they feed on garbage."

Rick replied, "That's right and worms and parasites."

Ellen asked, "What does it mean when they huff? I came on a female and two cubs when I was on the Appalachian Trail, a big female standing in the middle of the trail with her cubs and huffing away at me. I backed off. But then hikers came from the opposite direction, around a curve. They couldn't see her so I pulled out my whistle and warned them. The bears were gone in an instant.

"They can disappear like 'black magic,'" Rick grinned. Then he went on, "Be careful of berry bushes. They love berries and thickets. They'll ambush you in a thicket."

From the back of the room Bill Weitzel spoke up. Bill lives on property he owns inside the Park near the Stone Tower. "Hardly a day goes by I don't see a bear in the Park. And I never heard of a bear attacking a human here. You just have to be smarter than the bear. I used to run a meat market in town. Fellow came in one day and I cut him a nice big sirloin steak. Came in again later in the day and said, 'cut me another of those sirloins.' I asked what happened to the first one. He said, 'Darned if I know. Last I saw a bear was running off with it hanging out of his mouth.

After the laughter died down, Bill declared. "Never had an animal of mine killed by a bear."

With that, Roberta chimed in from the second row, "Friends of ours kept a goat in a shed. One night a bear ripped a wall off the shed but left the goat. They called the DEC and the officer said it looked to him like a man had done it. But to satisfy them he brought a giant bear trap. The bear came back the next night, tore off the rest of the wall and took the goat off with him."

Rick said, "The DEC trapped a troublesome bear up in Cain Hollow. I went up there to look. He had spread garbage all over the place."

Someone in the audience laughed, "The story is that when the DEC can't get rid of a nuisance bear, they trap 'em and then let 'em go over by the Reservation. The Indians are pleased to shoot 'em."

Rose Budnick commented in her polite way, "You don't see bears in the Park since they got rid of the dumpsters and centralized garbage collection."

I said, "I've read that there have been surprisingly few black bear attacks in New York State and almost no deaths, except for an infant a few years ago. But that over in Canada there have been quite a number of fatal black bear attacks."

Rick said, "Yes that's true about New York. In 2006 an infant was left alone in a stroller in the back yard. The bear was probably attracted to the baby's formula or his diaper. Should never have left the baby alone like that.

Black Bear Anesthetized
Courtesy of Seneca Nation of Indians Conservation

"Most of bear problems are caused by the way people handle garbage. In British Columbia they kill 1000 nuisance bears a year because people don't take care of their garbage. The bears get blamed and the bears get shot."

Bob Schmid had been listening and he burst in passionately to deliver this list of incidents in which he thought excessive violence had been used by Park Police on Allegany State Park bears. "In 2003 a Park Policeman found a yearling bear in the picnic area late at night. It wasn't bothering anyone. No one was there. He shot it repeatedly with rubber bullets. They're supposed to shoot them in the rear end but one of these bullets hit the bear in the heart. Some kids found him in the creek next morning.

"In 2006 they shot another yearling bear.

"2010 a female bear nurturing five cubs broke into some cabins. They went after her; shot and killed her. The police found only four of the cubs. Didn't seem to care about the fifth."

Berry Picking

Someone else in the audience intervened, "The police have a set of guidelines they have to follow. A bear gets three chances before they call him a nuisance bear. If he is in the wrong place they are supposed to adversely condition him by shooting him in the rump with rubber bullets. Trapping bears and moving them doesn't seem to work. They just wander back"

I added, "We need to cut the Police a little slack on this. If we have just one serious bear accident in the Park we are going to be very sorry. Maybe we need a legal way for people to get a look at bears."

Bill Weitzel said, "We used to have a zoo."

Rick Roth stepped in and ran through both sides of the argument but laid a lot of responsibility on people. "I've seen where a lady poured honey on her cabin porch rail so the bears would come and lick it off while she took their pictures."

The group responded with ironic laughter and Rick Feuz, our Program Chair, took advantage of the pause to take the stage. He stepped forward with a plaque bearing the images of two black bears. He thanked our bear expert and we applauded enthusiastically.

LOST
LARRY BEAHAN

June 2011

"For I'm a wise egg, I can lie steal or beg and I've traveled this world all around.

I been East, I been West and I'm there with the best when it comes to covering ground" ...but I got lost in Allegany State Park.

Larry Beahan on Colorado's 14,000 foot Mount Harvard

I'm an Eagle Scout. I've bushwhacked 25 miles from Stillwater to Wanakena across the Adirondack's Five Ponds Wilderness. I've taught mountaineering for the National Ski

Patrol, climbed Mount Marcy, Mount Katahdin and a couple of fourteen-thousand-foot peaks in Colorado. What the heck, I've been up Mount Fuji and I didn't get lost till Allegany.

June 11 I was in the Park for an Allegany State Park Historical Society Weekend. A friend and I decided to take a little walk, not a hike, just a little stroll into the 350 –year-old hemlocks off ASP 1. I'd been into those big trees twice before with Bruce Kershner who was an expert on old growth forests. I should have remembered that he got lost in there once.

Creek into Big Basin's Old Growth Hemlock Forest

About 2 pm we told Rick Feuz at Camp Allegany exactly where we were headed and where we would park the car. We laughed as we told him, "Come get us if we aren't back for dinner." In the back of my mind there must have been a feeling of extra security since my friend, Jerry Sultz, who is a member of the Western New York Search and Rescue Team, told me that the Team would be in the Park that weekend, doing practice searches. But I had no conscious idea they might have to look for us.

The route of our walk was simple, just follow this creek till you get to the big trees, take some pictures, turn around and follow the creek back to the road. But there are a lot of big trees till you get to the really big ones. The terrain is full of moss-covered boulders, downed trees and is cut up by small creeks feeding the main stream. It is dark and beautiful.

Big Old Hemlock

After forty minutes we had gotten our pictures and turned around to head back up-stream or at least that's what we thought we were doing. We looked for unique, familiar features but all the trees and boulders looked the same. We decided that somehow we had walked further downstream instead of up or that we had walked up a wrong tributary. We turned around again and walked and walked, clambering over rocks and around giant fallen trees, crossing brooks on and on. Still nothing familiar appeared. Our compass was of no use because we had neglected to bring a map and did not have a clear idea how the road related to our trek. A bushwhack east might have taken us into the road or into a vast wilderness.

Nothing Familiar in Sight

The day was hot and humid. We were dripping sweat. My lightweight cotton shirt soaked through. My liter of water was gone in no time. Our pace slowed, we stopped to rest frequently. About 6:30 we admitted we were dead lost and exhausted. We had contradictory theories about how to walk out. I thought we should retrace our route once more looking for something familiar. My companion thought we should bushwhack away from the creek toward where we believed the road might be.

Our fatigue dictated a compromise and we followed the standard advice to those lost in the woods. "Make yourself comfortable and wait to be rescued." So we sat down on leaves in a flat, relatively dry spot and waited. It was a few minutes before my companion noticed that we were surrounded by poison oak. We moved our bivouac several yards away.

We had not prepared for a "Hike." On a "Hike" there are ten essential things you must bring: map, compass, flashlight, food, extra clothing, rain gear, shelter, first aid kit, knife, fire-starting equipment. With them we might have built a shelter, lit a fire, made supper and rested in relative comfort.

I had only four of the essentials: compass, flashlight, first aid kit and a knife. I carried them in a small back pack that provided me some insulation when I sat on the damp ground. I also had along a very loud whistle which we used liberally. Cell phones are not very effective in Allegany's rugged hills.

It got dark quickly and soon I was shivering and experiencing muscle cramps, symptoms of salt and water depletion. We huddled together for warmth, exchanged life histories and finally tried to sleep. From time to time we heard car horns blowing and shouts. We answered with our own yells and three blasts on the whistle, the universal distress signal. We hoped those were the shouts of people looking for us, feared they were just people having a Friday night out.

The woods were pitch black. We decided that no one would chance a broken leg looking for us in this rough country until daylight. I slept a little, shook a lot and dozed off. About 10:30 I woke to hear more shouts. We responded with the whistle and our own shouts. Their shouts came closer. Then lights from head lamps approached through the woods. I lit my head lamp and they were there. Jerry and the WNY Search and Rescue Team were smiling, cheerful and happy to have found us, probably not quite as happy as we were to be found. They plied us with water and candy bars, checked to see that we had no broken bones and then carefully following their GPS equipment led us out of the woods. "Out of the Woods," what a wonderful expression.

You cannot imagine the relief, the joy that flooded us as their lights and shouts approached and we realized that we would neither spend the night nor eternity in this spot. I like Allegany a lot but I was not ready to leave my bones there.

Jerry Sultz, Member of Western NY Search and Rescue Team

Epilogue: Rick Feuz, Bob Schmid, Jay Wopperer and some others back at Camp Allegany noticed we didn't show up for supper. They alerted the Park Police and mounted their own search until they were shooed back to Camp. The Police called in the Search and Rescue Team and notified our families.

I spent the night at the Bradford Hospital where two bags of intravenous saline, some sleep and a good breakfast revived me. My son Teck and wife Lyn took me back to Camp Alleghany to exchange stories with the crew there, and then they took me home to rest up.

The Historical Society weekend went very well with plenty of eating, drinking, songs, a big campfire and our adventure to add a touch of excitement. Everyone had a good time, well, almost everyone.

Larry Beahan No Longer Lost

I hope I have learned the lesson of the ten essentials. In any case, just to be on the safe side, I have taken a note from rock climber friends. Now if I have to leave my car to go into a store, I belay a line off my front bumper and tie the other end around my waist.

SKIING IN ALLEGANY
SANDRA, LANCE AND LARRY ANDERSON

June 2011

Edna Northrup, Larry, Lance and Sandra Anderson, Ted and Terry La Croix

On this unusually warm May day the Historical Society met in the old grocery store on the Quaker Run side of Allegany State Park. The store has been turned into a museum. Our subject was skiing in the Park. I don't think Rick Feuz, our program chair, scheduled it for our cool comfort. More likely this was the only date on which he could put together this stellar line-up of Park ski-champions: three Andersons, Sandra, Lance and Larry, our speakers, and to keep them honest, Terry and Ted LaCroix and Edna Northrup. The Andersons and LaCroix's were born and grew up in the Park. Lance still lives there over in Bay State.

Eighty-four year old Edna Northrup, one of the founders of the Holiday Valley ski resort, had just returned from climbing to the 18,000-foot high Everest Base Camp.

Lance Anderson, actually all three Andersons, are solidly built and not above average height, a configuration that provides a sturdy stance for flipping through slalom poles at high speeds. Lance, or "Lanny" as Bob Schmid refers to him, took the floor enthusiastically, wearing a sport shirt and with his sunglasses perched on top of his head. He has a big authoritative voice and is obviously accustomed to public speaking.

My notes are pretty sketchy so take what you see in quotes, with a grain of salt.

Lance Anderson

Lance began by introducing his son, Ben, a younger version of himself but wearing a beard and an earring. Lance said, "This skiing and doing crazy stuff runs in the family. My son spends his winters in Steamboat Colorado jumping off 100-foot cliffs to make a living."

Lance had his frowning son stand on a chair and demonstrate the scar from his recent knee surgery. Pointing to the scar Lance said, "This cost me $8,000. We got him repaired. Now he can go back out there and jump off some more big rocks."

Ben Anderson

I think it was Bob Schmid who called out, "Wouldn't it be easier to buy him a parachute?"

Lance then turned to Bob and said, "When I first met Bob Schmid he walked up to me at my home, here in the Park, and handed me a package. It had our wedding picture in it. I didn't know what to make of him. I thought he was a stalker."

The crowd laughed.

"My sister, Sandra, called and said, 'Bob Schmid gave me a package. Is he a stalker?'"

This got a laugh and a half. After which Lance admitted, "Bob is the most knowledgeable person on Park history that I know.

"I am the Judge here in Red House. With 32 permanent residents we are the smallest town in the state but with the Park here we have one of the biggest courts. We run 1200 cases a year.

"So if you get pulled over on the way out, smile, take the ticket, say thank you and come see me." He winked broadly at us leaving us unsure where we would stand in such a case. He clarified this with, "You know what to do when you see a 25-miles-per-hour sign in the Park?" He answered. "Go 20. We gave 300 tickets last year for seat belt violations. It's worse here than in Orchard Park.

"Jay Carr (a member of the numerous Allegany Carr clan) is the most frequent defense counsel in my court. Hoping he might get on my good side, he once said in court, "This is the only judge who ever carried me down a ski hill on his shoulders.'

"He worked on restoring the ski-jumps. We go back a long way.

"Us kids living in the Park spent the whole winter on the ski hill. It honed your skill. Skiing in the Park started out on the Red House side at Bova. There was a rope tow to get you uphill. It was powered by a Chrysler straight six engine along with the original transmission. When we cranked it up you could really fly, lose your teeth. It was dangerous.

"Later they built a Poma lift over in Big Basin. It had a round plastic plate attached to a pole that you put between your legs. A big spring connected it to the overhead cable. When we were loading skiers, if you held it back just about 4 seconds, a cute girl would go sailing up through the clouds.

You'd go up and dust them off and say 'See you by the ping pong table in the Ad Building about seven?'

"In the mid-sixties you could ski on weekends all day long for fifty cents. Today up in Ellicottville it costs you fifty-four dollars. Fifty cents may not sound like much now but it was worth something then. We Park kids got together and went up to the Administration Building to see Lee Batterman, the Park superintendent. He was there in his white shirt and big belly. We told him 'Fifty cents is too much.'

Bova Rope Tow
Courtesy of Bob Schmid

"He said he'd take it up with the Park Commission. A few days later he called us upstairs and said, 'You ski free. You pack the snow on the hill for us so you ski free.' "We lived in the Park. We had no basketball courts or gymnasium. We were woods kids.

"At Bova, there was an older guy named Franz who used to get in a tuck position at the top of the hill and go straight down never making a turn, looked like a gooney bird, run over anyone in his way. One day after Sharpie announced, 'Last ride', Franz got up there ready to go. He didn't know it but the Park sanding truck had just laid sand down behind the warming hut. He came down that hill at fifty miles an hour, hit the sand and his skis came to a dead halt, didn't move three inches. He dug a trench with his jaw.

"The warming hut was at the base of the hill and there was a two-hundred-and-fifty-gallon drum behind it. The UB kids would come down to ski on weekends. They wouldn't know how to turn. One would go by; Sharpie (a Park policeman) would say 'Listen.' And 'BONG', another skier would hit the drum.

Charlie Dach's Bova Snack Shop
Courtesy of Ted La Croix

"The Bova rope tow was fast. Whenever I see a new skier with a big scarf I tell them 'Take it off.' I was in the safety hut at the top watching. This kid, with one of these long scarves around his neck, comes whipping up the tow. He goes through the safety gate that took 2 seconds to shut off. He was hung by the scarf 15 feet up, head to the right, poles hanging down by their straps. He had hung himself.

"I never carry a jack knife but I had one that day. I cut his scarf off him. I think I cut him. I thought he was dead. Someone caught him. Someone else pushed on his chest. He took a couple deep breaths and vomited, then rested an hour and a half and skied the rest of the day. There was no law suit.

We applauded and then Lance called his sister, Sandra, up front. She was ruddy-faced, smiling and had been busy laughing about old times with the LaCroix's and her brother Larry. Sandra said, "Sometimes Lanny can talk himself silly. That business about Mister Batterman's fifty cents was a big con. We never paid to ski. That's why I don't ski anymore. I can't see paying fifty-four dollars just to go skiing. I've got a ninety-pound daughter who is a rock climber. Competitiveness is born in us. If I ski I want to do it better and faster, not just for pleasure.

Sandra Anderson

Sandra quickly turned the floor over to her brother, Larry Anderson. Larry began, "There's not much left to say. Skiing is a whole different thing now. Carl Farner and Art Roscoe started skiing in the Park. They were both Park

Foresters. They built the two ski-jumps. The Park never had a formal ski budget. Carl and Art had Park personnel do the work and a lot of volunteers.

"I was very young at the time but I recall what Art told us about it. He used a team of horses to pull earth down off the hill and make the in-run for the jumps.

"The first ski-jump competition was in 1935. Ski trains came from Buffalo and Cleveland. Flint and Kent, the Buffalo Department Store, organized ski tours. Bus loads would come. There were ski repair shops and small hotels. Skiing really boomed after World War II and the money was welcome down here.

Larry Anderson

"In Red House, the LaCroix's and the Boyers boarded skiers in their homes. Sarah Rank and her husband turned their house over to twenty skiers and moved into the woodshed for the winter. Sarah made them breakfast, a box lunch and had a big roast beef or turkey dinner. You could order a reindeer sweater from her on Sunday and she'd have it all knitted for you by next weekend. It would take my wife all winter.

"While I was in school I worked on the ski tow with Art Roscoe. Then I worked for him in the Park and on the weekends I ran the tow.

"Skiing went like that here in the Park until about 1950. Then Ellicottville, Glenwood and Kissing Bridge took over. Many of our skiers volunteered for the 10th Mountain Corps. They trained in Colorado. The 10th Mountain Corps spent three years fighting in Italy but never did any skiing. They got into mountains but not on skis."

Red France in Downhill Race Big Basin 1957
Courtesy of The Buffalo-State Courier Express Collection

Larry slowed down for a moment so I asked, "Did you do any cross-country skiing in those days?"

Ted LaCroix stood up to answer, "Larry used to make me ski from Bova to the Administration Building. I got so good at it that I won a few cross-country races. We used to ski Ridge Run down to Bova in 35- 40 minutes and have someone pick us up with the truck. A bunch from Paul Smith's and from up around Watertown came down, a really good ski team. They'd do that run in 19 minutes and be waiting for me when I got there with the truck."

Sandra said, "There were a number of ski clubs in the area who would host races. They would add up the race results to keep score for the year. Our team from the Park was called the Inter-State. We had a lot of good skiers. The opposition didn't like to see us coming."

Larry stepped in again, "Bova opened in 1940. It only had 250 feet of vertical but it was a nasty little hill. Our downhill race course was the hardest in the country. Every time I went off I'd hit a tree, did quite a lumber job. Sandra was our forerunner. She was short, fast and close to the ground.

"We skied with the long thong and bear claw binding. We didn't want the foot to come out. It was a choice between breaking your upper leg or your lower leg.

"Our 30 and 50-meter jumps were the only all-natural jumps in the country for a long time. The others all used towers. In 1956 over 10,500 people came to watch a jumping event. Franz Elsigan broke the previous record of 163 feet with his 188-foot jump. When he landed he shattered the tips of both skis

Larry wound things up with, "The Niagara Frontier Ski Council elected me president one year. The next day I got my draft notice. That shut down my skiing for a while."

Sandra got in the last word by demonstrating a metal clamp that was popular for a while for a better grip on a rope tow.

The crowd applauded enthusiastically as Rick awarded all six skiers with plaques and we took historic photos of this crew of Allegany ski racers.

ALLEGANY MAMMALS
WAYNE ROBINS
April 2009

Wayne Robins with Silver Fox Pelt

Wayne Robins stood before us stroking the beautiful grey and black pelt of a silver fox. He had beside him a barrel of furs and a table covered with plaster animal tracks and bottles of scat. "Scat is animal poop," he soon informed us. We were assembled on a sunny March day in one of the classrooms at Camp Allegany. The warmth of that day after a cold night had the maple sap running in the sugar bush outside.

Wayne was dressed in nineteenth-century woodsman gear; wool knickers held up by suspenders over a wool shirt. He had a big red handkerchief sticking out of his back pocket and an old plug hat waited for him over in the corner. He was loaded and primed to teach us the mammals of Allegany State Park and immediately afterward to teach maple sugaring to a bunch of grammar school kids.

Wayne and Judy Thaler are partners in Nature Ed-Ventures. They continued running the Buffalo Museum of Science's Allegany Nature Education program when the Museum reorganized. Wayne had worked for the Museum many years here in its Allegany operation and in Buffalo as an adult educator and preparer of exhibits.

"Mammals have always been my hobby. I've been working on this collection all my life," he said sweeping an arm at the table of specimens. This morning in Camp we woke up to a serenade of coyotes. Down here one time, a BOCES class teacher came in all excited. He had found a kill site. Usually it's no big deal; just a few feathers left over from an owl kill. But this was something different. There was blood all over. There was a tangle of drag marks and bloody footprints, guts, skin and bone. A pack of coyotes had killed and eaten a deer. Some hunters would say 'Damn coyotes, what a horrible thing.' It was horrible, but it was natural. I'm a hunter too. But I'm a guest in the woods.

"When I do a 'Mammal Survey,' I look for what they left behind, their tracks and their scat."

Tracks

"No tracks are perfect. For example, a red fox is supposed to have nails, four toes and a heel pad with a chevron shaped callus, but you rarely find one exactly like that. So if I find a good track I make a Plaster of Paris cast of it. You can buy plaster of Paris in a hardware store. I go to a lumber yard for 50 pound bags. Last year I used seven of them. Had a lot of cast classes.

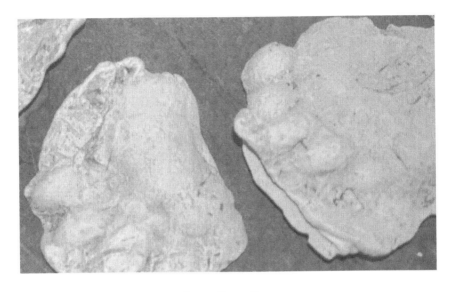

Bear Paw Casts

"To make a cast, take a container, a coffee can with a snap-on cover is good. Put the water in first; otherwise plaster lumps up. Add a little plaster at a time and stir until it just drips off the spoon. Pour the mix on the track. It hardens in half-an-hour but give it a good hour. It's easy to do. A big mistake is to not write down where you collected it, like, 'Allegany, April '09, half mile up Red House Creek from boat launch.' You learn quickly.

"How do you tell a dog track from a coyote track? The first rule is, never say, 'always' or 'never' because, next time will make a fool of you. Say, 'usually.'

"A dog's track is usually as wide as it is long. Its claw marks are spread out, relaxed. He's overweight and out for fun after a big meal. A coyote's track is narrower than long. His toes are together with two toenails straight ahead. He's not lazy. He doesn't run around to sniff at every interesting thing like the dog. He goes straight into a thicket or where the food is. He will follow a snowmobile trail for half a mile looking for half a candy bar...and because the trail is easy to walk on.

Wayne passed around two plaster casts, one of a great blue heron and the other a turkey. "I got this turkey track on a three-mile hike with Terry Dailey, the Park Forester. It was a cloudy day and I wanted to hurry it up because it was beginning to rain. I poured the plaster quickly without really examining the track. When I got it back here I found that, besides the turkey, I had possum and mice tracks. It was like the mice were having a town meeting. There was one place that led in and then thousands of little tracks milling around inside a small area. You get surprised like that. Once I thought I had a porcupine track. It turned out to be a snapping turtle.

Wayne Robins leading a Hike

"I had 50 grammar school kids on a hike and 'Whoa,' there was the track of a 400-pound black bear. He had just stepped in a puddle and dropped a lump of still steaming scat." Wayne passed around the cast of a huge bear paw. He did not tell the story of how he and the 50 kids escaped the bear. I assume the bear was scared-as-the-dickens and scooted out of there as fast as he could.

Scat

Wayne then grinned, "I'm infamous for scat collecting jokes." And again he failed to tell us one. I just took it for a warning.

He moved on to deer scat, "Everyone knows deer scat, right? But how many deer are responsible for a particular collection of scat. It may be 17 different scats from 17 different deer; one ate green grass, another blueberries, a third juneberries and one of them had diarrhea from eating green apples."

"Eleven to twelve-thousand years ago during the ice age, cave dwellers in Northern Spain and in France set aside toilet areas. We've examined their mummified scat and found out what they ate and from the pollen count what the climate was like.

Food scraps

"Animals leave food scraps behind. There is a 60-70-pound beaver at work nearby in Red House Brook. He leaves stumps and chips. Rabbits cut branches at a 45-degree angle because of their big front teeth. White tail deer have sharp lower teeth but no upper front teeth. They grab a branch and twist their head making a 180-degree cut.

"In high school I spent a day with a game warden. We had had a hard winter and a farmer had applied for a damage permit to kill deer because they had destroyed a number of trees in his orchard. We went in and found the branches were all cut at 45-degree angles. Rabbits had done the damage standing on their hind legs on top of deep snow."

Beaver

Wayne made this emphatic statement, "Two animals can change habitat to improve it for themselves... man and the beaver. The difference is that the beaver also improves it for a lot of other animals.

"It is fascinating how beaver work. They live in ice-covered ponds digging tunnels into the bank. They dig underwater and then come up inside the bank above water level. Or they build a lodge of sticks and mud and always with a thin area on top. You can tell in the winter if a lodge is active. Ice forms around the air hole on top.

"Beaver store branches underwater in the creek for winter food. They can stay under water 10 to 15 minutes. Their metabolism slows down. They have a membrane that covers their eyes, flaps over their nose, the ears close, heart slows down. They use 75% of the oxygen they inhale. We use only 15-17%.

Beaver Tail

"If he gets cabin fever in the winter, a beaver can come out of his den and swim 15 minutes under the ice. He extends that by finding bubbles under the ice to get an extra breath. He can make himself a breathing space by exhaling under the ice and re-breathing his own air to use up the 25% of the oxygen he had left in it. He can do that 3-4 times.

"A beaver has to constantly groom to keep his fur clean in order to stay dry. Otherwise he'd die of the cold. He has oil glands on his abdomen and both hind feet have split toenails that you might think came from injuries but they are there so he can comb out burrs." Here Wayne picked up a beaver paw to demonstrate the split toenail.

Wayne Robins on a Beaver Outing

Squirrels

"Rodents love to chew. A squirrel can chew up a Pepsi can. Red squirrels are the most dangerous. They chatter, stamp their feet and act really sassy. I watched when my aunt and uncle parked their pickup under a pine tree. A couple of red squirrels were throwing down pine cones that landed in the truck. My uncle moved the truck and when the two squirrels came down, they were furious standing there stomping their feet arguing, angry." With squirrel-like tones and movements Wayne acted it out, "Who stole my cones?"

"A squirrel will eat its own poop to digest bark pulp better. It comes out in mucous-covered pellets.

Lou Budnick spoke up. "How come you see black squirrels in Canada and only grey ones in Buffalo? "

"Wayne answered. "It's the same species, just a different color phase."

Lou said, "I need a couple red squirrels to chase the greys out of my yard."

"Red squirrels can't even live with each other," Wayne said. They'll drive the birds away. I dumped feed into a bird feeder all one fall. A red squirrel chewed a hole in the metal bottom and it all fell through. I was fit to be tied. My daughter said 'You can't shoot them.'

"Well, I was home alone with a 22 with a scope on it. I threw a handfull of seed out on the ground. The red squirrel came out and was gobbling them down. He was bobbing in the scope and out. Then a grey snuck in, took just one seed and stood off to the side. The red stalked him and then jumped on him and chased him. The grey was like 'I didn't do it.' And the red was jumping around like, 'I can't believe it,' and going 'hmmm, hmmmm' human like. I couldn't do it. I couldn't shoot a crying squirrel.

<u>Pelts</u>

"I'd like to show you my collection of furs," and he reached down into a barrel and started demonstrating them one by one. "They are valued by color and texture. I made this study-pelt when I was sixteen. It is fourteen inches long. Ordinarily weasels are 10-12 inches. Down south they are all brown like this one. In Pennsylvania half of them are brown and half white. In Alaska and Canada all of them are white. If you take southern weasels to Alaska in a few generations they will all be white. It depends on the amount of light they are exposed to. We raised some at the Museum and they were random brown and white."

He showed us a longer dark-brown pelt. "This is a mink; this year's largest ever, 30 inches. When I first saw it I thought it was an otter. A mink is a semi-aquatic animal with a straight tail. Bushy tails are useful for balance in bounding around tree tops like this Adirondack pine martin does. He has this orange patch under the chin.

"The DEC has been stocking river otter around here. An otter is in the water all the time. He is a quick predator with no body fat. His hair is very thick, a million hairs per square inch. He can swim a quarter-mile underwater and dive to 150 feet.

Red Fox Black Color Phase

"This pelt is from a fisher, he said, holding up a blackish-brown fur. Despite their name they do not live near water or eat fish. "Fisher" comes from the French name for a similar animal, the *fichet*. They have suddenly appeared in

Western New York. They do best in mixed coniferous and deciduous forests eating red squirrels and birds."

Grinning, Wayne produced an unmistakable black and white pelt. "I don't need to tell people what this one is. Other names for them are civet, and pole cat. Down south they are spotted instead of striped. Skunks are nearsighted. I have a picture of Grace Christy and a line of little ones close together following their mother. They don't hibernate. It had been a mild, open winter and they had no fat. Grace Christy was up dangerously close taking her picture.

"The badger is an animal that not even a bear will challenge for food. His hide is thick and loose and he is low to the ground and muscular. If a dog bites him he will spin around inside his hide and bite the dog's face. A naturalist once did a study where he followed a badger at a distance every day till he tolerated him. He watched as a coyote approached the badger and got snarled at but the two walked off alongside each other. The badger sniffed a ground squirrel and started digging him out. The squirrel ran out the other end of its burrow and the coyote got him. Then vice versa. The Naturalist thought it would never happen again but he told the story to a class and a little kid said 'I saw that on Animal Planet.'

"The Iroquois call the muskrat 'little brother of the beaver' but say they don't like each other.

"In the 1920s and 30s possum were rare around here. If someone got one, they'd show it off. Now you see them all the time. During the same time cardinals have moved north. Possums are active mainly at night, but when flooded out of their dens may be seen in the day. They eat everything including insects and they love road-kill, therefore they often wind up as road-kill themselves.

"You all know the raccoon with his blackface.

"The grey fox is the only true North American fox. Canines and felines split from a common ancestor. Felines have retractable claws, therefore no claw marks in their prints. Canines run prey down. Felines hide and spring out with switch blades exposed. The grey fox is between the two.

"During colonial days they tried English fox hunting but the grey fox climbed trees to escape. He wouldn't cooperate. So they imported the red fox in the 1700s. The Hudson's Bay Company, the first fur company in North America, has records back to 1622. The red fox doesn't show up in them till the late 1700s.

"In the 1920's everyone looked for a silver fox. A silver fox is a color phase of the red fox. Out of a litter, four kits may be red and one silver. If you mate two silver fox, you may get a red. All red foxes have a white tip on the tail."

Looking for Mountain Lion Tracks

Wayne handled delicately a beautiful white pelt. "I could have sold this Artic fox many times. They follow polar bears around hunting seals. The bear waits on the ice at a seal breathing-hole. With one swoop of a paw, the bear kills the seal instantly. He eats the skin and the fat and leaves the rest, for the fox. The bear needs a high energy diet. He will never kill a goose. It would cost him more energy then he would gain.

"This is an eastern coyote skin from Great Valley," he said handing around a large yellow-brown pelt. "I grew up with rumors of coyotes. The rumors gradually evolved. The first story was that dogs were breeding with western coyotes and what we were seeing was coy-dogs. That never really happened. DNA testing tells us now that these are Eastern Coyotes, a separate species.

"The forest has grown back and the coyotes that were hanging around the periphery have recovered. They are related to the eastern timber wolf. The DEC tried to reestablish them in the Adirondacks but they wandered back to their home in Canada.

"In the Park, we have 3-4 sightings of fisher a year. Coyotes are all over the place.

<u>Mountain Lions too</u>

"The mountain lion, panther, puma and cougar are all the same animal just called different names depending on what area you are in. In Florida and the east they run about 80 pounds, out west 100. Not long ago, one was killed crossing a road at night in the Adirondacks.

Wayne pulled it all together and left us on a hopeful note with this on mountain lions: "We thought we got rid of them all, but cats are secretive and adaptive creatures, like coyotes. A few have survived on the fringes. They'll be back."

SENECA SNOW SNAKE

November 2004

Michael Crouse is one of three Allegany Reservation Senecas who practice the art of making snow snakes. The Iroquois National sport is the hurling of these six-foot, spear-like missiles down a ten-inch-deep, mile-long icy trough, for distance. It has been proposed as an Olympic event.

Michael Crouse 2004

On a cold, overcast November day, 30 members of the Allegany State Park Historical Society gathered in the paneled great room of the Red House Administration Building to hear Mike describe how he makes snow snakes and how the game is played. He is a tall, good-looking man in his fifties. He wore jeans and a collared gray sweatshirt. His eyes and dark complexion are Seneca though the Crouse name comes from a distant relative, Peter Crouse, who was a European hostage, later adopted into the Seneca Nation.

Mike and his Daughter Kate

Before his talk, Mike confided to me, "I'm so nervous I can't stop sweating, this is the first time I ever spoke in public." It may have been his Seneca blood, but as he spoke, he seemed perfectly poised while I had flubbed his introduction by forgetting to say he had been a logger, was a carpenter and used to travel with his dad who played a lot of snow snake. Mike conducted the session more like a conversation than a speech. He made frequent comic asides and took time to answer questions. He laid out ten snow snakes, the most prized of them coming from a foam-lined pool cue case. He started by saying, "The guys call these, 'sticks.'"

While Mike talked, his daughter, Kate, put on a soundless video so we watched an actual snow snake competition as we listened to him. The video was a forest scene with fallen leaves, bare trees, snow and frozen mud. Men in woolen hats and jackets took turns. Each grasped a "stick" in one leather-gloved hand and ran at a hip-high ridge of snow where, underhand, they hurled the sticks down a long, long icy groove carved in the top of the ridge.

Here is what Mike had to say about it:

"We lived in Onoville, till they flooded the Kinzua Reservoir in 1964. Then we moved to Steamburg. Snow snake kind of died out after the move but now it's come back to where it was. There are several teams here on the Allegany Reservation. Some reservations have 10 or 15. They play all over. Every weekend. Travel to Syracuse, into Canada. Whoever has snow calls a game and are the hosts. There's lots of joking around. But it's serious.

"When I was 10 or 12 my brother used to take me out in the woods, I called it 'Child Labor' then. We took a crosscut saw. We'd cut logs into 8-foot lengths and then into boards and then inch-square or bigger sticks. We'd take them home and use a drawknife. You had to be strong enough. A few of you look like you know what a draw knife is."

(We called it a draw shave in my family. It is a two-handled knife you   pull toward you when carving a piece of wood fastened in a vice.)

"Old fellow named Jack Henhawk used to live with us winters. He made snow snakes. He was legendary. Had an old cabin in the woods. Stayed with us in the cold spells."

Mike picked up one of his snow snakes. "Make them out of Rose, Zebra, Cocobolo. Look for a pretty wood, nice grain but a wood that will work out, too. Apple is good, if you can find some long and straight enough. Hickory is long and has all the qualities you want. Maple and cherry, too. Years ago some guys colored them with food coloring. This one is apple. Hold it one way, see the grain, another and it shifts." He demonstrated the grain of the slim, brown rod he held.

Mike demonstrating an Apple Stick

"Basically, I'm a carpenter. Rebuild houses and do some furniture. When it comes out straight you feel proud."

He hefted the stick. "Apple is something …to work with. I picked this up the other day and it had a bow in it. It's straight today. Effected by temperature and humidity. Maple and hickory stay straight.

"I been making them 10 years. Last three years, I been playing but I don't travel.

"Every stick's a little different. You try a certain style. Then the wood takes over and makes it come out its own way."

Mike picked up a green-colored stick for our inspection. With its expanded head and metal snout it looked a great deal like a snake, perhaps a snake with rigor mortis. "Juneberry, this one here," he said. "You look up on the hill in spring and it is the first flowers you see. White, like dogwood. But apple is heavy. Most are heavy. The theory is, heavier the better."

Tom Quinlan stood up and asked, "How do you throw it?"

Mike Demonstrates How a Snow Snake is Held

Mike said, "Come here. Here's how you hold it." He showed Tom the notched butt end of the snake, around which Mike hooked the last joint of his right index finger. The next few inches of the stick were balanced on the tips of his other fingers and amazingly he was able to support the remaining six feet, extended out in front of him. Holding it like this, with only that hand, he passed it to Tom who tried that grip but quickly brought his other hand into play exclaiming, "No way!"

With a little practice most of us were able to hold these six-foot-long, 11-to-17-ounce, and flexible rods with one hand in the prescribed fashion. Whether any of us could throw one a mile or even get it into the slot, remains to be seen.

Someone else asked, "How do you surface them?"

"Normally I use shellac cut with alcohol. Sand it off and repaint several times. Takes eight to ten hours work and the dust ain't too good for you. To sell, I use shellac; for myself, I boil in oil.

"Each guy brings several sticks to a game. Some have forty or fifty. Depending on snow, ice, sunshine, cloudy they pick a certain snake. Each has his own wax, like on skis and no one will tell. Some oil them and use only certain oil. Some soak it in oil. Some put it in a pipe with the oil and use an air pump to pressure-treat it. There is certain furniture polish oil that the EPA didn't like, so now you can't get it anymore. I bought it up. I get my wax from Holiday Valley."

Bob Schmid asked, "What about the metal tip?"

"I melt tire weights for the tip," Mike said, picking up the largest of his sticks, a pale maple one, well over six feet and a good solid inch in diameter. All the rest were more like a half-inch thick. He smiled and said, "This is Big Berta," showing us the name carved into it. "I made it mostly to get attention. Teams put different names on their sticks so when you go down the track you know whose it is.

"I had a chunk of metal, worked real well. I found it along the Pennsy track. No one knew what it was. Maybe part of a train brake. It's all gone now. You melt it up. Then pour it into a cone around the tip. You have to file it down to shape. It's soft so if it starts to rattle you bend it."

"What are the rules of the game?" I asked.

"The teams are usually two men. Each team puts up 10 or 20 dollars and gets four throws. The farthest throw wins a point. Whatever team gets four points wins the game and the money. A team can win on the first throw if all four of theirs are farther than everyone else's. If it's getting dark they might have a sudden death round and farthest throw takes all."

"Do women come to the games?" came from somewhere in the audience.

"They're only allowed if they bring the food." The audience laughed and let it go while Mike described the food. "It's mostly something quick, maybe chili-dogs, coffee and donuts, fried bread."

Then one of the younger girls asked, "How come women can't play?"

Mike hesitated a moment and seemed embarrassed. He said, "I just found out yesterday. But I can't go into it here. My daughter, Kate," and here he motioned to Kate who glowed. "She's pretty good at it but she only plays when it's just me or some friends around."

Larry Beahan Handles a "Stick"

"How do you make the track?" Jim Carr wanted to know.

"Used to be with shovels, now they use a snow plow. Pile it up about hip-high, then take a sixteen-to-twenty-foot pole about ten inches thick and drag it to make a track. Some wrap it with barbed wire so it will dig in. They pour water on to make ice."

"What is the longest throw?" someone asked.

"Longest I ever heard of was about a mile and an eighth. If they need to make the track longer they do."

"What's the technique?"

"It's mostly all in your arm. You walk back from the trough and mentally see where your feet are going to go. If you slip, you stop and restart. Most wear baseball spikes. I don't. My knees bother me. They're not ready for a quick stop.

"Some days you can't miss. Some days you can't hit a thing. I'm quiet out there but some guys, especially the guy who has the point, will get up and holler and scream and haggle and jeer to try to throw the next guy off, break his concentration. There's no cussing but they'll yell, 'Go, go, go get the money… or something.'"

Bob Schmid said, "I notice on the video that guys will run down the track twelve to fifteen feet. Is there a foul line?"

"No, there's no foul line but guys will holler at them. Your own team marks how far you throw but you better get it right .You can't get away with anything. You win by inches."

"Does anyone ever get hurt?" Bob went on.

"The snake is going up to ninety miles-an-hour at the start there. You want to give it ninety degrees on either side. I got hit once as a kid. You learn quick. Some have to get yelled at."

"Is everyone welcome?" Tom Quinlan asked.

"Sure. A lot of Non-Nations play. Never throw anyone out."

We thanked Mike with a round of applause and then gathered around his table to handle the snow snakes and ask more questions. I got him aside to ask about the prohibition of women at the games. He said, "It's because women might be menstruating and it would frighten the men."

Mike makes souvenir snow snakes that sell for around sixty dollars, game quality sticks go for eighty dollars. For beginners and kids he makes three-foot-long models called Mud Cats.

Senecas host snow snake games on winter weekends in Allegany State Park at the Stone Tower near the Summit Cross-Country Ski area. Beginners play on Saturday. Only the first and second-raters play Sunday. Mike promised to give me a call when the next game is scheduled and I will spread the word.

ALLEGANY SKI CHAMPION EDNA NORTHRUP

July 2008

In 1948 Edna Northrup won the Nagle Memorial Slalom at Allegany State Park's Bova Ski area. At eighty, she skis all winter and in the off season, she hikes to the top of Holimont ski slope three times a week, "I do it because I want to ski," she told us.

On a green and sunny July 19th, sixty years after that ski victory, Edna addressed the Allegany State Park Historical Society at St. John's-in-the-Woods Chapel. Slender and vigorous, she was formally dressed for the occasion in a royal blue flowered skirt and a plain white blouse set off with a silver pendant.

Old friends of hers like Ellen Gibson from Foothills Trail Club and Lanny Anderson, the Red House Judge, were among the crowd to whom Lou and Rose Budnick served iced tea and brown-sugar-walnut delights called "Blondies."

"Skiing is woven into the fabric of my life," Edna began, with a bit of a rasp in her voice. It became apparent as she told the story, that she was a pioneer of skiing in Western New York and that skiing is the predominant pattern and one of the most important materials of her rich life.

"In 1941 when I was fourteen I saw the movie, 'It Happened in Sun Valley.' It was the first time I saw skiing. It excited me. Skiing has never left my mind since.

"The first time I went skiing I went to Allegany with friends. Diamonds sparkled in the snow. A fire blazed in the fireplace of the Administration Building. The Bova ski hills, tucked back into the woods there, were so beautiful."

The Bova ski slopes remain well-preserved in the forest at the western end of Red House Lake just behind Camp Allegany. The old rope tow is not there but, in winter, if you are willing to walk up, you can ski.

"I graduated from high school in South Buffalo in 1943. Mother bought me skis boots and poles for $25. It was tough for her. That was a lot of money. Today the same equipment would cost $2500.

"I wanted to be a Forest Ranger but women weren't allowed, so I went to work. Mother was the Post Office clerk at Weed And Company and she got me on there. Flint and Kent, nearby, had a ski department headed by Andy Hengsteller, the 1928 Olympic ski-jump champion. He advised me about equipment and told me about people in Ellicottville who helped me with skiing.

Edna Northrup at 20

"No one else I knew caught the ski bug. I would take the train from downtown Buffalo and pass through all the little towns on the way to Allegany. Down there I met my good friend Lillian (Russell) Congdon and we skied together for years and years. I earned twelve dollars a week, gave five dollars to Mother and still had enough to stay in a hotel. Skiing cost twenty-five cents.

"At Bova, I learned to turn on skis and after that I could handle myself.

"That was 1944-45, the end of the war. Bill Wilson bought Camp Tall Spruce at Bova. I was always a very good swimmer. I had Red Cross Lifesaving so I went to work for Wilson as a swimming counselor. His friend, Bill Northrup, the Ellicottville dentist, had been in Africa and Italy for three years. Bill Northrup came home; we met there and got engaged that summer. We married in September 1946.

"Skiing began in Western New York here at Allegany. I got proficient at it and got into racing along with Lillian Congdon at Bova. We had Gangs Hill in Salamanca and Dipple Hill in Bradford. The equipment wasn't what it is today. We used hot tar and wax on our ski bottoms. The metal edges came in sections that you'd buy in a hardware store. Every day you had to replace some of the sections.

"To make those skis turn, you had to really move your body. Now you just wiggle a little.

"Too bad Bova had to close. It had that old rope tow. Your arms used to get pulled longer. Later we had that 'Platter Pull' over in Big Basin. Now 10-12 thousand people a day ski at Holiday Valley on groomed slopes. There are lots of accidents. A local man was killed this year.

"I cross-country skied with Bill Wilson and his wife. We'd build a fire and make tea out in the woods. That was before our friend, Art Roscoe, built the excellent cross-country ski area up at the Summit.

"Two or three women and I learned to Telemark. When Bova was closed we'd go there and use the fresh powder.

Lou Budnick asked, "What is Telemarking?"

Edna answered, "It is a kind of skiing they did thousands of years ago. You turned your skis by advancing one ski ahead of the other. That brought you around in a wide slow turn. Back then they used one big pole instead of two. We tried one pole. It works better with two."

I asked, "Have you tried snowboarding?"

"Don't even like the look of them," she snapped back. "I know the learning curve is shorter on snowboards but there are bad injuries with them."

Allegany Ski-jump 2007

She went on, "All my life I've come to the Park. When Lillian got so she couldn't walk well, we came down bird watching. We kept a list of all the animals we saw."

Someone asked about ski-jumping.

"In the beginning there was ski-jumping. There'd be a thousand, sometimes two thousand people watching. It was international. People came from a distance. A lot of people from Cleveland came, just to watch. Some stayed overnight at the Ad Building."

Bill and Edna Northrup

Bob Schmid said, "The Allegany jumps were considered the best in the country."

The sites of those ski-jumps are visible on the hill above Red House Creek just below Red House Dam. To find them, take the service road that goes below the dam. You will see them to the left in a short distance.

Edna picked up on Bob's remark, "Allegany was important in skiing history and at Ellicottville Bill Wilson and my husband, Bill Northrup, and I were an important part of it. Lillian and I have written a book *For the Love of Skiing* that tells all about that. Bob Schmid gave us so many pictures for it."

"Where can you buy it?" someone asked.

"I have a few with me but I didn't come here for that."

The Internet tells us that in 1956 Bill Northrup, Dick Congdon and John Fisher decided to pursue their dream of opening a larger, modern ski area at Holiday Valley. Shares of stock were sold for $100 from a card table in the parking lot in 1956 and 1957, 4 slopes were cut and a T-bar was built. A mild early winter delayed opening until January 7, 1958 when the first skiers rode the T-bar up to ski down Yodeler, Champagne, Holiday Run and Edelweiss.

"I hiked the 111 highest peaks in the Northeast, did the Long and the Appalachian Trail, been an outdoors person all my life."

Ellen Gibson asked, "Do you still hike with the Foothills Club?"

"I maintain seven miles of trail through Ellicottville," she replied. "The Finger Lakes Trail goes all across the state and connects with trails across the country all the way into North Dakota."

Lyn Beahan asked, "Did you ever visit Sun Valley, where they made that movie? And didn't you think that hill was pretty dinky?"

Edna responded, "Yes," then went on, "Bill and I and another couple went out there, we weren't married yet. The war was just over and it wasn't open. We climbed up to the Round House and skied down.

"It was a privilege to raise kids in a wonderful small town like Ellicottville and be a part of all this. We cut off skis for the kids and used tuna cans for heel pieces. They were all skiing by five or six."

Bob said, "Your daughter, Penny, was quite a skier."

"She was six years on the U.S. National Ski Team. She won in Europe. We used to drive 20,000 miles a year when she was competing and still in school. Sometimes we'd have ten kids in the station wagon."

Penny Northrup Racing at Allegany's Big Basin
Courtesy of The Buffalo State Courier Express Collection

Bob said, "In 1948 you won the Nagle Memorial Race. You and Lillian seemed to have had a lock on the sport."

Edna said, "We had specialties. I won the Slalom and she'd take the Downhill. I used to tease her that it was because she was heavier."

For a few moments, Bob Schmid and Lanny Anderson held forth on prominent skiers associated with the Park and debated Park ski-jump records.

Then Edna summed it up with. "Back then 219 was just a dirt road. We always drove down 242. Forests grew up over the ski-jumps. We've got signs up to indicate where the old ski-jumps were. Otherwise they'd be forgotten."

Bob asked, "How do you feel about the changes in Ellicottville?"

"I was mayor for eight years. It was a town full of vitality and young people. But people with normal jobs can't live there anymore. There are no kids, so we have no schools. There used to be 1200 full-time residents, now we have only 500. Taxes are horrendous. Very few attend our Episcopal church. The Pastor is 95. Times are tough. $4-5000 is too much to pay for taxes. They've just put up a condo that looks like a prison. Each unit costs $5-600,000. And they are not selling.

"Once when I was hiking in the Smoky Mountains, I saw a Forest Ranger all dressed in green and leading a string of pack mules. I thought a moment about how I used to want to be a ranger, then thought, I have had a very good life. I have a daughter, a gynecologist, who writes best-seller books. I'm a widow thirty years. I sold our house to my son, Calvin, and built a cabin on a pond in the back in honor of my daughter Cindy who died at 23. She worked on the Alaska pipeline and was killed in the storm of '77.

"I'm in my own cabin now, my most favorite place to be," she said with a wistful smile, and then added, "If I can't be in one here in Allegany!"

Edna Northrup fell in love with skiing and with Bill Northrup. Together they built careers and a family out of snow country and skiing. She is not about to quit.

Edna Northrup's lesson is, if you get a chance to do it all over again, do more skiing.

PART THREE

PLACES

ALLEGANY AUTUMN
LARRY BEAHAN

October 2010

On the way to an Allegany State Park Historical Society outing in the Park, Lyn and I took the I-90 and exited at Irving on the Seneca's Cattaraugus Reservation. It was a good day for that route to the Park since the intention of the outing was to explore Tunesassa, the site of the former Quaker Indian School. Tunesassa, on the Kinzua Reservoir, is now the Park's Friends Boat Launch. After that we would join the Senecas for an Indian Thanksgiving dinner in Jimersontown on the Allegany Reserve, just outside the Park.

Seneca Hawk at Irving

Once the Senecas owned all of Western N.Y.; now they live on three narrow reservations. On this trip to Allegany State Park we had an opportunity to review some of the historic changes to the Allegany region, experience some of what has not changed for a long while and to ponder the effect.

In Irving, we stopped to fill our tank with tax-free gas at Seneca Hawk, a combination gas station, restaurant and cigarette shop. Then Route 438 took us the length of the Cattaraugus Reservation. The sun shone in a blue October sky making green fields glow and illuminating woods in red and gold. I felt awe, entering this sovereign nation, and leaving our own, especially now when there are strong differences of opinion about the collection of taxes.

Fall Foliage on the Way to Allegany

We passed neatly kept houses and mobile homes and then the modern Cattaraugus Reservation Administrative Center. Things looked more prosperous than I recall from similar trips in recent years. The sale of tax-free gasoline and cigarettes and the casino business seem to have benefited this community.

Route 62 led us out of the Reservation and through the village of Gowanda, which is our usual jumping off place to visit Cattaraugus Creek and Zoar Valley. Today we sped through it into Amish country. There, time has stood still. Weathered barns and tall silos of traditional 19th century farms spot the roadside. In a broad green field two straw-hatted farmers, each behind a team of horses combed the sod into brown rows, the old-fashioned way.

Pumpkins for Sale

The Amish, for all their simple ways, are eager to engage in business. Frequent hand-lettered signs advertise wares and services: baked goods, quilts, hand-made furniture, a "tarp shop."

In Randolph, shortly before reaching the Park, we found a roadside stand full of fall harvest for sale: pumpkins, squash, gourds and barrels and barrels of apples. They also sold ice cream from a modern freezer. We split the difference between new and old and enjoyed their specialty, a giant hot-caramel-apple sundae.

Then, on to the Park, where thirty-five of us gathered for the Allegany State Park Historical Society meeting in the Quaker Store Museum. The Museum is located on ASP Highway 3 in Quaker Run. The meetings are open to the public so there were a number of new faces as well as many old familiar ones with deep roots in the Park.

Kenny Watt attended the Quaker Indian School at Tunesassa

Among those present who had survived changes that we would consider were: Kenny Watt was a student at the Quaker School in 1937. The school closed a short time after he left. Pete Smallback was present as well. He grew up at the

Tunesassa site. Pete's father bought that former Quaker School farm. Pete's 90-year-old mother was there with him and his wife, Carolyn. Carolyn was born in Corydon only a few miles down the Allegany River. Corydon has been underwater since the river was dammed in the 1960s to make the Kinzua Reservoir. In the 60's the Park expanded and forced the Smallbacks off their land.

Bob Sieben, dispossessed resident of Allegany's German Village

Bob Sieben was there to show us the site of "German Village." His family joined several others to build that rustic cabin colony just outside the Park not far from Tunesassa. Three waitresses who worked in Charlie Dach's Red House Inn, a family who camped in another cabin colony called Buzzardville, and three brothers born on a farm that is now

Park, were all in attendance. Tunesassa, Buzzardville, German Village and the Red House Inn all have given way to Park expansion. Those who were displaced still express regret and loss but these Park veterans love their Park.

The Quaker Store Museum, where the meeting convened before our tour, was not built by Quakers but by the Larkin Company to supply groceries to campers on the Quaker Run side of the Park. It is now the Park museum and is stocked with memorabilia including a stuffed bear, hundreds of photos and a mock-up of an original Allegany-style cabin with an iron cot and wood stove.

After a brief business meeting we proceeded in a twelve-car caravan to the Park entrance on ASP 3 at Quaker Lake. There, Bob Byledbal took over. Bob grew up in the Park concession business under the tutelage of his parents. Later he took over the management of the Red House dancehall and store. He is full of stories of square dancing, rock and roll, and the kids who worked for him in the Park.

Bob Byledbal at Race Track, now a Meadow by Quaker Lake

Bob met us in a wide meadow near the lake. Pointing at a pine tree some distance off he said, "Not many people know it but this was a stock car, dirt racetrack and that was where the driveway entrance was, right by that tree." Bob described the popular, noisy, dusty place it was in the early 1960's. Park expansion ended that era. Surprisingly, there was also auto racing on the ice on Red House Lake until warm winters and thin ice ended that.

Our caravan moved from Quaker Lake west on ASP 3 to Tunesassa on the Kinzua Reservoir. There we gathered behind Pete Smallback's pickup truck parked by a grove of trees while Pete handed out Xeroxed photos of the old Indian School buildings and described the place and its history.

Foundation Remnants of the Quaker Indian School, Tunesassa

In the 1790's Chief Cornplanter asked the Philadelphia Quakers to build a school in Seneca territory. Three Quakers, the first white settlers in Cattaraugus County, responded by establishing the Quaker Indian School that survived here into the 1940's teaching European-style farming and the "Three

R's." At the time it closed there was a large school and dormitory building, several cottages and a 450-acre farm with a huge barn.

The day before Pete and a friend had prepared our way by cutting a path through the brush and into the trees. We followed the path to the banks of the Kinzua where a bit of concrete rubble still marks the site of the main school building. He gathered us there and told us that when his family farmed Tunesassa the main building was gone but they used the barn for their dairy herd. Under the barn floor they found a small cellar where turnips may have been stored. Pete believes that room was used to hide runaway slaves who had come up the Ohio and Allegany on their way to freedom in Canada.

Pete Smallback and his Mother were forced off the Tunesassa Farm

Pete led us back to the truck where he made it clear that he and his family were badly treated when the government ordered them off the property to make way for the Park. Kenny Watt, the only Seneca present and an actual student of the school, had very little to say but he must have had many thoughts about the fruitless Seneca battle against the Kinzua Reservoir that flooded a third of the Allegany Reservation.

Some of the group followed Bob Sieben to the German Village site but it was dinner time and our contingent had reservations for the annual Thanksgiving dinner put on by the Senecas of the Jimersontown Presbyterian Church.

Salamanca and its casino are on the Allegany Reservation, the only Indian reservation that hosts a city. Jimersontown is a suburb of Salamanca. This year the meal was served in a new ultra-modern Seneca Nation of Indians Administrative Building there.

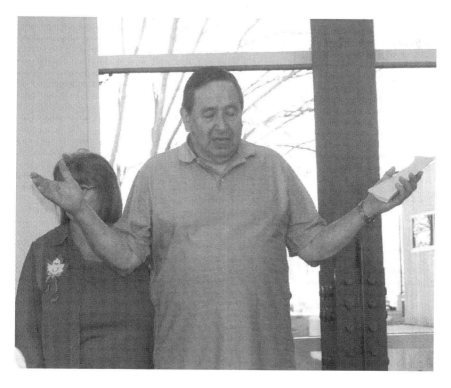

Thanksgiving was offered both in Seneca and English

Broad arching windows look out the back of the building's dining hall. They provided us a magnificent view of Allegany Reservation hills covered with maples in flaming colors. Before dinner was served the church Pastor led us in a simple hymn in English and then he taught us to sing it in Seneca. The meal was of turkey and venison with fried bread and the three sisters of Seneca agriculture, corn, squash and beans and, of course, pumpkin pie.

As we left by the building's front exit, satiated with food, history and natural scenery, the giant Seneca Allegany Casino and the Golden Arches of Salamanca's McDonalds confronted us. I shrugged in resignation and supposed the Senecas, too, would prefer their scenery unspoiled... except for the prosperity.

A BRIEF HISTORY OF ALLEGANY STATE PARK
BOB SCHMID

March 2011

It was March. There was still snow in the Park. The ice-covered lake dominated the view through the French doors of the great room in the Administration Building. Rick Feuz, on short notice, drafted Bob Schmid to replace our scheduled Historical Society speaker who canceled because of illness.

Rick Feuz and Bob Schmid in the Red House Administration Building Great Room

Rick introduced Bob, covering the fact that Bob was one of the founding members of the Allegany State Park Historical Society, probably knew more about Park history than anyone and that he would tell us the story of three buffalo who once roamed here.

Bob took the floor. He is a great big, tall fellow who looks more and more like one of his beloved Allegany State Park bears every year. He began with, "I know Rick announced that I would talk about those three buffalo that escaped in the Park but I could do that in fifteen minutes and be all done. So I brought along a selection of pictures, maps and articles to show you and I made up these packets you can take home." Here he handed out ten-page stacks of materials. He said, "I'm going to tell you the history of Allegany State Park."

And by golly, he covered a heck of a lot of that history in the next hour and a half. Nobody has the memory for Allegany dates and stories or the archives to back them up that Bob has. I will try to sketch in the outlines of what I heard and add a few thoughts of my own.

Instead of three buffalo, Bob produced three Allegany State Park maps 1927, '28 and '29. He began, "The 1927 map was only of the Quaker Run area where the Park started. Its legend shows Remington Trail, named for one of the Park's first superintendents, Cyrus Remington. Today we have with us that superintendent's grandson, Dave Remington."

Dave, sitting in the front row, waved an arm and the audience of 30 or so Historical Society members laughed and applauded.

"Camp Turner and Camp Fancher are on the 1927 map and Lookout Trail is shown up behind Camp Remington.

"The 1928 map shows the Administration Building in Red House. If you'll notice, a 'Proposed Lake' is indicated where Red House Lake is now. On the Quaker side of this map, Camp Kosciusko, the Polish Boy Scout Camp, is shown on ASP1. You had to drive your car through the creek to get to it. I always wondered how you got back if there was high water."

Bob Byledbal hollered, "Plenty of beer."

Bob Schmid chuckled and went on, "Camp K was torn down in 1954. Some of the cabins were sold and moved to private land to be used as rentals."

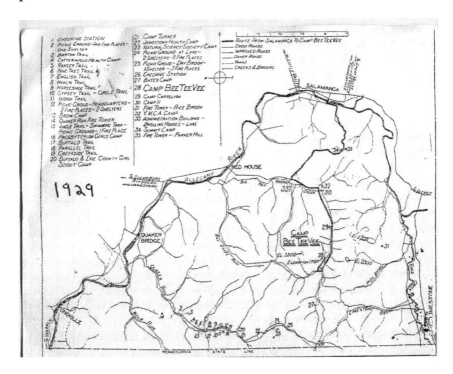

1929 Buffalo Turnverein Map of Allegany State Park

"The 1929 map was sponsored by Camp Bee Tee Vee, the Buffalo Turnverein Camp which is now Camp 12. Larry and Lyn Beahan gave us a tour there last fall, I believe they worked there and had their honeymoon there."

I called out, "Bob, the Bee in Bee Tee Vee is for Beahan."

My wife Lyn put up her hand and asked Bob, "On that map, would you show us where the Fancher swimming pool was located?"

Larry and Marjorie Beahan at Fancher Pool 1934

Allegany State Park Historical Society at Camp 12

  He answered, "Fancher pool started as 'The Mud Hole,' a dammed-up creek left by the Tunesassa Lumber Company across from the rental office. The first concrete pool was 40 by 80 feet and built there in 1926. In 1934 a new one was built down ASP3 across from the Fancher Cabin. It was replaced in

1955 and closed in 1984 when Quaker Lake Beach opened for swimming."

Someone asked about Legion Trail. Bob answered, "That was the American Legion Camp. It was across from Ward Trail. Lou Budnick's family had one of the cabins there as a yearly rental. It was way up on a ridge and the pump was at the bottom, making a trip for water kind of tough.

"In the handout, you've got Larry Kilmer's map of gold mines in the Park and a bunch of newspaper articles from 1896-1901 about the mines. They never produced much gold. One of them was in Bay State over behind Beck Hollow, another on the Patterson Railroad in Bova and a third was near the Summit close to the Red Garter Restaurant."

Then we saw what we had come for. Bob showed us a blown-up photo of a buffalo taken from an old post card, not this one but this will do. He said, "In 1931 two men named Swieger and Gordon opened a horse concession in the Park. They planned an 'Old West' style dude ranch equipped even with a prairie schooner to give rides around the Park. At that time, the JN Adam Tuberculosis Sanitarium at Perrysburg had a zoo for their patients. It was so expensive to feed their three buffalo, the largest land animals in North America, that they had to give them up. The Sanitarium offered them free to anyone who would take them.

"They fit right into Swieger and Gordon's plan. They borrowed the Holt family's old barn near the Park to house the male and a female adult buffalo and a calf. The calf was bigger than any animal in the Park. On November 30th the buffalo burst through the barn wall and through a fence. They roamed loose in the Park until May 1932. They were in Cricks Run and Quaker Bridge. Up into Red House where they stopped a train. Down in Bradford dogs, cars and police chased them back into the Park. They broke into the Quaker Farm corn cribs and ate all the stored corn.

"The mother buffalo died in a snowstorm in March and was found frozen on a hill. It was illegal to hunt them. Deer slugs were no good. Finally they got an OK from the authorities to use a 45-caliber rifle which did succeed in bringing them down. The meat was donated to a home in Machias."

There was no obvious response from the audience. We all pretty much knew the sad ending but were fascinated to hear these details of how it played out.

Bob shifted gears and pulled out a rare poster-sized photo of the crossroads at the center of the tiny village of Red House. He said, "This scene was located about at the center of what now is Red House Lake. In August 1929, those buildings were either torn down or moved below the Dam. The Town Hall lasted there on the old maintenance road till the winter of 2010 when the roof caved in and this wonderful historic building had to be torn down.

"In the spring of 1930 Anderson Trail was built by Park Maintenance at the rate of one cabin per day. In 1940 Dowd trail was built. People ask why Dowd was so inconveniently located, up on a ridge. It was because, at the time, the ridge offered a fantastic view of Red House Lake. It's overgrown now."

I called out to Bob, "My family liked Dowd trail because the cabins had electricity and because we could walk from there, to the beach." That was my contribution to Bob's history of the Park. Rick Feuz added, "My Dad and his friends loved those cabins because it was such an easy walk to the dancehall."

Then Bob rolled out statistics. "Allegany State Park has 65,000 acres. That's 98 square miles. In Quaker Run there are 22 cabin trails and 221 cabins. Red House has 7 trails and 155 cabins. There are plans for a thousand campsites and so far there are 164.

"Allegany is spelled three different ways: A-l-l-e-g-h-e-n-y in Pennsylvania, A-l-l-e-g-a-n-y in New York and A-l-l-a-g-a-n-y in Maryland.

"In 1920, all the New York State Parks were in the eastern part of the State. Albert Fancher made a lot of money in the oil business and lived in Salamanca. He got together with Hamilton Ward and General Charles Adams to see what they could do about a Park in their western end of the State. They went to talk to Governor Nathan Miller in Albany and he thought it was a great idea. He said, 'I'll put up $25,000 of State money if you can match it.' On the train home they agreed to put in $5,000 a piece. They persuaded others to chip in the rest and they purchased the first 7000 acres of the Park for $50,000.

Andy offered, "The Holland Land Company donated 7000 acres back at the start."

Bob didn't comment but went on, "The Park opened in 1921 and the first accommodations were World War I surplus army tents. In 1924 they built wooden walls for the tents and in 1927 the cabins were completed with wooden roofs."

He mentioned that the Salamanca Historical Society had information on Fancher. "They are really quite an organization. They have three floors of materials in a building across from the bank."

Kings Row Park Employee's Housing

Rick Feuz stood up to add, "The old Fancher Mansion in Salamanca has been turned into a church. The Historical Society is planning a *Stars of Salamanca* celebration and is doing a whole exhibit on Fancher."

Bob took a deep breath and said, "Feel free to make announcements or ask questions. I know I stand up here and am such a wind bag. My wife says I just like to hear my own voice.

I'll agree, Bob is a talker but he has a lot of information and I love to hear him talk.

He brought out his collection of photos of the Administration Building during its construction. Passing the first one around, he said, "Here is King's Row when it was new. It is those four houses up behind the Administration Building where Park officials live.

"The Administration Building was put up in 1927 at a cost of $148,000. It is 238 feet long by 48 feet wide. The second floor, which is now occupied by offices, started out as hotel rooms. On August 4th 1929 the restaurant on the second floor served its first meal, a full course turkey dinner. From 1944 to 1973 dormitories were set up on the main floor during hunting and skiing seasons. The third floor started as a storage area and now houses offices. Last year the Park put a new copper-flashed slate roof on the building for "$240,000. Just imagine what a new building would cost today.

"There are three lakes in the Park, all man made. Science Lake was the first. Built in 1926, it was used for swimming until there was a death. The old diving platform is still there. When they were pouring concrete to build the 22-foot-high spillway that would control the water in the lake, Louis Remington was the foreman on the job. One of the wooden forms containing fresh cement gave way accidentally. His nephew, Jason Remington, a laborer on the crew, was buried in it. Fortunately they pulled him out quick and he survived.

"Louis sent Jason home early and the story is that Jason's mother had to use a tweezers to extract the cement and pebbles from his ears and nose. Come payday, Jason noticed that he was short two hours of pay. He complained to his grandfather, Cyrus Remington, the Park superintendent, 'I almost lost my life, how come you docked me?'

"Cyrus responded, 'You don't work. You don't get paid.'

"December 1, 1930 the 33-foot-high spillway for Red House Lake was closed. The average depth rose to six and a half feet. The Lake covered 120 acres; 30 times the size of Science Lake and it covered the site of the village of Red House.

Lyn Beahan and Jay Wopperer at Red House Spillway

"In August of 1964 the 48-foot-high spillway of Quaker Lake was begun. Two-hundred-and-seventy-five acres of some of the best farmland in Cattaraugus County were covered in water averaging 27 feet in depth. Originally the Lake was to be called Tunesassa after its location near the Quaker Indian School but because Tunesassa was thought too hard to pronounce they called it Quaker Lake.

"It took 5 months to fill the Lake. We know the date exactly because former Historical Society member Roland Remington's family farm was near the spillway and Roland's mother recorded in her diary, "At 6:30 AM on November 21, 1968 the first drops of water went over the Quaker Lake spillway."

Girls at Quaker Lake Beach

Bob ended his talk with that story and we gave him an appreciative round of applause.

Bob Byledbal interrupted the applause by honoring Schmid with a resounding, melodic, baritone rendition of "Give me a home where the buffalo roam and the skies are not cloudy all day." We poured on more applause and laughter.

HELLBENDERS AND WALLEYES

November 2011

My experience with Walleyes has been limited to the gustatory. They are a very tasty menu item that I particularly enjoy pan-fried. I have never even considered eating an Allegany Hellbender. I saw one once a long time ago in Red House Lake and he looked neither handsome nor delectable. George Heron, a former President of the Seneca Nation, told me they used to catch a lot of them in the Allegany River and just threw them back. He said, "Some old-time Indians used to say, 'Hellbenders got a devil in 'em. They're poison.'"

I looked up Allegany Hellbenders a while ago, and learned that they live only in the Allegany and Ohio River systems and that they are the largest Salamander in North America. They can grow to 29 inches and can live 70 years. Hellbenders thrive in swift clean waters and are valued by Senecas as a symbol of purity.

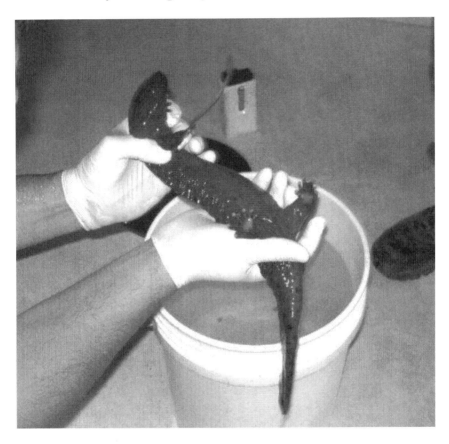

Allegany Hellbender at the SNI Hellbender Rearing Facility
Courtesy of Seneca Nation of Indians
Fish and Wild Life Department

Allegany Hellbenders seemed to me iconic of Allegany State Park, so I called my first book about the Park, *Allegany Hellbender Tales*. I was eager to hear about the Seneca efforts to encourage Walleye and particularly Hellbender reproduction.

The Seneca Nation of Indians Fish and Wildlife Service invited the Allegany State Park Historical Society to tour their new Walleye fish hatchery and Allegany Hellbender rearing program. We must have a very high percentage of fishermen in the Historical Society because this tour attracted fifty participants; one of our largest turnouts.

SNI Conservation Officer Clayton Ludwick at SNI Fish Hatchery

Clayton Ludwick is Conservation Manager for the Seneca Nation. He brought along two other SNI Fish and Wildlife Service Officers to our meeting in the Red House Administration Building. The three were dressed in the distinctive khaki and black fatigue uniforms of the Service.

Clayton took a few minutes while we were still gathered in the Administration Building to describe their operation, "The Seneca Nation received a grant from the US Fish and Wildlife Service to fund our Walleye and Hellbender programs. Walleyes are-over fished. Hellbenders used to be very common around here and now they seem to be dying out.

"The hatchery building that we put up for Walleyes is a 'GREEN' building. We are totally off the grid. There are 26 solar panels on the roof and we have 24 battery packs that store enough electricity to power the building for four days. It is a steel-paneled building with a heavy coat of insulation applied to the interior. Our water supply is gravity fed.

Historical Society at the Seneca Fish Hatchery

"We have ten hatching jars and plan to double that. When we are fully operational, we will be releasing two million Walleyes annually. Fingerlings and the slightly larger fries will be released at different times of the year.

"The New York State DEC has been generous in educating our staff. We've made field trips to their facilities and we are copying their style of operation. In the off season we have collected trees and placed them in ponds and in rivers and in the Kinzua Reservoir to provide protection for small fish. We use SCUBA gear to photograph those sites and make sure they get used. We plan to recapture some fish to check their survival rate. We are trying to educate fishermen to throw back female Walleyes and that Hellbenders are not at all dangerous to people or harmful to fishing so they should throw them back, too. The Allegany River is shallow. There are silt beds where fish get landlocked. We plan to address that with dredging."

Clayton stressed the point that these facilities would be open to the public daily from 8 to 4:30 and he urged us all to come back, bring friends and sign their registry books. "It helps our funding," he said.

Fish Hatchery Sign

When he finished Rick Feuz gave driving directions. "Go toward the Red House exit. Just past the Church, before Route 86, you take a right on a paved road. It is a dead end.

The only road off of it is a gravel road to the right. Follow that to the hatchery. When we are done there, we will go up Route 86, get off at the Casino exit in Salamanca and take the RC Hoag Road, which is directly across from the Casino, turn left off Hoag onto Center Road. The Hellbenders are in a small white barn behind the Fish and Wildlife Building. If you are afraid of getting lost, follow me."

Historical Society at SNI Hellbender Rearing Facility

In the meantime Bob Schmid had gone around the room handing out a collection of newspaper clippings on the subject of Hellbenders. Some of the most fascinating articles were from the 1920's and 30's describing the Hellbender investigations of the Buffalo Museum's Allegany School of Natural Science.

Rick's directions to the first site were surprisingly easy to follow and at the hatchery our long stream of cars and trucks filled the parking lot and lined the road. The building itself is colored bright green which underlines the fact that the Hatchery is solar-powered. The array of solar panels and battery packs were displayed prominently. Two large rectangular ponds were located in a fenced enclosure to the right of the parking lot.

Clayton ushered us inside to see the glass hatching-jars and plastic fish-tanks for newly hatched fish. Water cascaded through the system but no fish. "We will be stocked with fish and operating in April 2012. The Walleyes we raise will be descended from local stock on the Seneca Allegany Reservation. We will go out into the Allegany River and use 'shock boats' to capture fish and bring them in here to milk them of their eggs."

The internet says, "A 'shock boat' – also known as a Model SR-18-E Electrofishing Workboat – is a motorboat with two long arms on its bow that dangle metal squid-like clusters of wires into the water. A gas-powered generator sends 1000 volts of electricity into the river. The jolt stuns the fish but is too mild to kill them."

At the last minute someone asked, "What does a Seneca fishing license cost?"

Clayton answered, "It's $45 and every cent goes to support fishing, including this operation."

Then someone else asked about the picture of a Paddlefish that was posted in the visitor's room. "Paddlefish used to be common around here," he answered. "They're an indicator species, an indicator of environmental quality. Some of them get to be six feet long. Their snout is the shape of a paddle and is about a third of their length. We have one in a bottle of formaldehyde and the skull of another at the Hellbender site. Be sure you get to see 'em."

Paddlefish
Courtesy of Seneca Nation of Indians
Fish and Wildlife Department

We all filed back to our cars and most but not all found our way directly to the little white barn that houses the Hellbender Rearing program. Those that were lost eventually made it. It was just as well that we straggled in because the building is suited for only about six visitors at a time. Clayton stayed outside answering questions and chatting with those waiting a turn.

While we waited I overheard someone say that up into the 1970s every August a Hellbender feast was held at Saint Bonaventure's. Then a woman, who said she was a newspaper reporter, said, "I heard that their skin was toxic. If you handle them and then touch your eyes they'll get inflamed."

Clayton confirmed her statement. "The mucous on their skin is mildly toxic. It's their only defense. It makes them taste bad to predators.

Allegany Hellbender and his Crab-dinner

Inside the building the program was in operation. A mature Hellbender immediately caught your eye. He was about 26 inches long, a mottled brown or khaki in color, lying quietly in the bottom of a glass fish tank, his long powerful tail curving out toward us. He was snuggled against a rock, his big stubby feet hanging motionless. His only movement was the slow undulation of the flap of skin that extended along either side of his abdomen between fore and hind legs. I read that this flap serves as a Hellbender's chief organ for absorbing oxygen. They also have rudimentary lungs and a single gill slit. You can tell them apart from the related but slightly smaller species, Mudpuppies, by their hind feet. The Hellbender has five toes and the Mudpuppy only four.

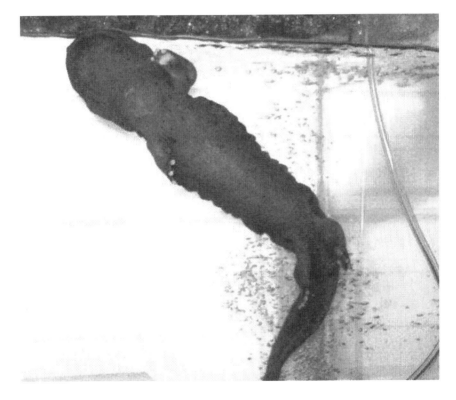

Hellbender
Courtesy Seneca Nation of Indians
Fish and Wildlife Department

On top of the rock sat an unsuspecting crawfish while two minnows swam around curiously staring back at us spectators. When asked about these other creatures the Officer said, "They're his dinner."

This Hellbender looked peaceful enough but as I watched him and his tiny eyes watched me, I recalled reading of the Hellbender's mating habits and imagined him in a swift moving stream jealously guarding the cave he had hollowed out beneath a flat rock so that other smaller fellows couldn't usurp it, as he herded chosen female Hellbenders into the lair, forced them to deposit eggs as he fertilized them and then expelled the poor spent ladies and searched for another mate and another until he was satisfied. Then he protected his brood of offspring till they hatched in 68-75 days, only occasionally gobbling one down-- to sustain himself.

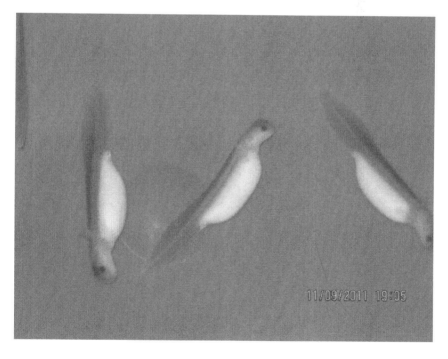

Tadpole Hellbenders
Courtesy Seneca Nation of Indians
Fish and Wildlife Department

Another smaller tank held ten hatchling Hellbenders in the larval or tadpole stage swimming about vigorously. A drinking glass on the table against one wall contained a live embryo still in its egg casing waiting till it was mature enough to leave. One of the Conservation Officers explained, "We collected these guys as fertilized eggs from under rocks in the Allegany River."

In a bottle on that table one of those weird-looking Paddlefish was displayed. It was about a foot long and was a good 30 % proboscis. Behind it on the table was the skull of a fully-grown adult of that species. The skeletal snout was the size of a small canoe paddle.

Officer Clayton Ludwick and Historical Society Members at Hellbender Rearing Facility

Outside, Clayton Ludwick continued to hold forth, "Hellbenders get up to 29 inches long. The biggest one we've ever had here was 28 inches. We collect eggs from the river and bring them to our Hellbender Rearing facility here to give them a head start. When they're about four years old we will return them to the river. We'll try different sites till we locate the best ones. It's a funny thing. Our best Hellbender site right now is in the Allegany River where Tuna Creek (Tunungwant Creek) comes in and that is about as polluted as you can get.

"There are a number of zoos with Hellbender Rearing Programs. The Buffalo Zoo is raising 540 Hellbenders. Recently they sent 40, in the larval stage, to the Bronx Zoo.

"Hellbenders have never been bred in captivity. We go to meetings with PhDs who have a lot of book knowledge but they may have handled only one Hellbender in their entire lives. My guys have handled 110. The Buffalo zoo has a great facility but they have constant lighting and constant water temperature. Here we vary the light exposure according to the time of day and the year. We have a guy check the river temperature every day so we can be just one day behind with the water temperature. When we start breeding we will have a circular tank with water moving through it like a stream."

Clayton declared, "It's a race. A lot of zoos are trying to breed Hellbenders. There is no reason why we can't be the first. We have all the knowledge and more experience."

NEW YORK STATE FIRE TOWERS

August 2004

Allegany's Summit Fire Tower 2004

This summer Paul Lasky made another trip to Allegany State Park. He is a great lover of fire towers and has devoted a big chunk of his life to their study and preservation. On his first trip to Allegany he climbed the trails to our Summit and Tuscarora Fire Towers to collect information and photos for his book, *The Fire Observation Towers of New York State - Survivors that Still Stand Guard.* When he decided to do a New York State fire tower book, there already were four of them on the market. To make his distinctive he visited every single fire tower in the State and photographed them all.

Fire Tower Lecturer Paul Lasky at Red House

Allegany State Park invited him this time to speak to general Park visitors but our Fire Tower Restoration Committee took full advantage and showed up in force. Paul did his slide presentation amid the turkeys and other wildlife of the Red House Administration Building's Natural History

Museum. He delivered a cascade of anecdotes, facts, figures and lore.

Paul explained that his interest in fire towers began when, five years ago, his hiking club, the Adirondack Mountain Club, started its Fire Tower Challenge. The Club was concerned about the overuse, literally the abuse, of the Adirondack High Peaks. There were so many hikers and campers in them that many of the trails to their summits were turning into muddy roads. To persuade hikers to use other parts of the Adirondacks they set up a Fire Tower Challenge. Like the "Forty-sixers" who climb all forty-six Adirondack Peaks that are over 3600 feet high, Fire Tower hikers would try to visit each of the 20-30 fire towers in the Adirondacks and 5 in the Catskills.

The Challenge worked. It moved people out of the High Peaks and put Paul to work visiting every tower in the entire state.

Paul wore a plaid shirt, hiking boots and dungarees. He is energetic and looks to be in good shape. This was verified in a brief byplay between Paul and Bob Schmid. Bob claimed climbing Tuscarora Mountain was tough. Paul called it easy and claimed the discrepancy in their estimates was because he hiked to a tower every weekend.

He showed us some great old pictures, turn-of-the-century loggers at work cutting timber and hauling huge loads of logs on sleds pulled by teams of massive horses. He made a point of the expansion that this country was going through in those days; the demand for iron and lumber to build cities. He showed us log jams on rivers with $2.00-a-day lumberjacks risking their lives prying them apart with peaveys. "Logging is the most dangerous job in the world," he said.

His pictures put me in mind of the family stories about my grandfather's logging camp on the Little River near Star Lake in the Adirondacks. I have a wood carving of Uncle Raymond's. It is a lumberjack using a peavey to hold his balance as he stands on a floating log. Raymond talked about Grampa carrying him on his shoulders and jumping from log to log in the river and Grampa bragging that he earned his pay

Uncle Raymond Beahan's carving of Grampa Tom Beahan as a river pig

even though he couldn't swim a stroke. I'll swear that carving was of Grampa.

Paul explained the often-neglected fact that a great deal of iron was mined and processed in northern New York. The ore was refined in blast furnaces that used charcoal. All and any kind of wood was burned for charcoal. With guys like my grandfather and his two brothers going hammer and tong at the Adirondack forest there soon was a quarter-of-a-million acres laid waste in the name of profit and progress.

Lumber barons bought great tracts of land and did as they pleased with them with no regulation. Loggers took no pains, as they do now, to cut the limbs and tops so they lay flat on the forest floor. Instead the "slash" was left in huge puffballs of aerated fuel just asking for a spark to set off a torrent. Sparks were easily come by. The Adirondacks were crisscrossed by lumber railroads that used wood-burning locomotives. Steam engine firemen opened ash-doors at 40 miles per hour and spewed smoldering coals along the track.

Pike Mason with an Early Power Saw

Fires became a big problem. John D. Rockefeller lost 50,000 acres in the early 1900s. Frances Webb learned the lesson. He owned the vast Ne-Ha-Sa-Ne estate where, in addition to having his own his own railroad, he had a personal fire department. In 1903, the year before my dad was born at the Little River camp, 64,500 acres burned at Lake Placid. It covered Albany with two to three inches of ash. New York City was shrouded in smoke for two weeks. People became as obsessed with and fearful of forest fires as today we are of terrorist attacks.

Trains were not the only source of fire. Wilderness ethics had not taken hold. Campers and hikers stripped bark from trees for lean-tos and left campfires burning. The Adirondacks had become attractive to tourists. People confined to cities suffered under crowded living arrangements in dust and coal-smoke. Rates of tuberculosis were high. People had been coming to the mountains for the good, healthful air and the uncluttered forest.

Maurice McDonald in an Adirondack Stump Field

Grampa talked about the "Sports" that came to the Beahan camp to hunt deer. He had a system. He told them,

"Keep Maple Mountain in view on your left shoulder as you circle. That'll wind you up back in camp."

Paul showed an early 1900 photo of a poor disillusioned "Sport" laden with an Adirondack pack basket and gazing across a moonscape that had been forest. People like him and Verplank Colvin made a plea to the New York State Legislature to take on the forest fire problem. Paul had a photo of Colvin in a suit, tie and hat sitting in camp with a couple of gnarly-looking guides cooking dinner for him.

Water quality became an issue. The cities in the watershed of the Adirondacks began to worry. The usual duff on the forest floor, so useful in holding rainwater and preventing sudden run-offs, was being burned away. Muddy water rushed out of the forests causing floods and then water shortages as the forest lost its ability to hold water. The potash that ran out of the woods in the water killed fish. Paul said, "After a storm townspeople could pick trout out of the water like potatoes from a field."

Between 1903 and 1908 there were a million acres lost to fire. In 1903 they fought one fire for three months. It did not go out until rain put it out. When the forest around Long Lake went up, the villagers of West Long Lake fled into the water. They described the sound of air being sucked into the inferno to be like the roar of a freight train. Up to their necks in water, they watched while everything they owned burned.

By 1908 the railroads were all required to burn oil instead of wood. Fires were then chiefly caused by fishermen and campers.

The US Forest, Fish and Game Service kept statistics on forest fires and it was soon apparent that Maine had much less a problem than any of the other lumber-producing states. They had developed a system of fire towers manned by fire wardens with maps, binoculars and telephones. Maine detected its fires early and instead of five or fifty thousand acres being destroyed they would lose fifty.

In 1909 New York began building fire towers all over the state. The first was at Stephentown. Paul had a picture of it, a simple wooden ladder to the top of a tree. At the base of the tower was a hand-cranked telephone for reporting to the fire warden. A variety of wooden towers were built but they rotted out in five to six years.

In 1915 the Aermotor Company supplied NY State with 10 light-weight steel windmill towers equipped with ladders. In 1917 they came out with one made of heavier steel and equipped with stairs and a roofed cab to keep the observer out of the sun and rain. The federal government contributed money to buy fire trucks and equipment like the 2.5 gallon backpack "Indian" hand pumps.

Fire towers were manned from late spring through fall for the fire season. Their cabs were supplied with an adelaide, a circular map of a 30-mile-in-diameter area on a table with a sighting device. If an observer saw smoke he took a bearing on it and telephoned the news to headquarters. Simultaneous sightings from several towers allowed for triangulation and the pinpoint locating of fires.

Alton, Raymond and Leo 1921
An Auto Camping Trip to Raquette Lake

The tower program, together with public awareness and modern logging methods, was effective in controlling fires. Paul has interviewed several veteran fire observers and their descendants. Some quite successful observers were women. In the 1970's fire towers became less and less necessary as several modern developments took place. The system of roads developed in the Adirondacks made observation and communication much easier. In the 1920's my dad, his brother and a cousin tried to drive the mud roads from Carthage across the Park. They had to turn around when the Raquette Lake Ferry demanded five dollars to carry their jitney across. If they had had a fire to report to the other side of the lake, it would have been tough.

The last working New York State fire tower, the one at Old Forge, closed in 1992. Some other states still use them but now in New York five men in airplanes do the work of dozens in towers during the 1920's and they do it at a fraction of the cost. Beside these official channels, everyone has cell phones these days and 90% of fires are reported by private individuals.

Paul has photos of all the existing New York State fire towers and many that are gone. He showed us a great number and variety of them, stone, metal and wood. He told stories of the rebuilding of many of them. Most of the work has been done by volunteers. He talked of the controversies involving others towers. For example, whether the Saint Regis Tower should continue to stand in what is supposed to be a wilderness, where no man-made structure is allowed.

Paul's home tower is on Hadley Mountain. I believe he had a tear in his eye when he told us, "The warmest moment of my life was when my son said he wanted to spend his twenty-first birthday at the top of Hadley Tower."

After Paul finished speaking and answering questions we took him along upstairs to a meeting of our committee in the stately room dedicated to Park Commissioners. There, with his historical background and previous career in building fire escapes, he was able to shed light on such things as how to handle the replacement of fire-tower diagonal braces. The ends of our diagonal angle-iron steel braces had originally been flattened so they could be bolted to the uprights. Now we have to replace those braces. Terry Dailey, our Chairman, mindful of the New York State Office of Historic Preservation's requirements on the Park, asked how this was done.

Paul said, "You could do that by heating them till they are red and then beating them with a sledge hammer. Originally they were probably done with a trip hammer in a metal-working shop. On Hadley Tower, where we don't have to be exactly historical like you do here, we just fastened the bolts through one side without flattening."

Terry Dailey Fire Tower Chairman in the Commissioner's Room

Paul's advice and encouragement have given our own fire tower repair an important morale boost. Volunteers have been fabricating steel braces and measuring bolts to replace. Soon we will need carpenter volunteers to fit new stairs in place. Not long after that we should be able to celebrate some birthdays high above Allegany's South Mountain in our own Summit Tower.

NEW IRELAND
PAUL LEWIS

November 2010

In November, Paul Lewis spoke to the Historical Society and told the story of New Ireland, the now-deserted Irish settlement near Limestone in Allegany State Park. He had told it to us several years ago but that time we rushed him through it so that we could hike to the site and see it with our own eyes. This time we were older, perhaps better focused and less interested in exertion. So Paul had an opportunity to tell a much fuller story.

Paul Lewis October 2011

He was dressed for the occasion in an emerald green polo shirt emblazoned with shamrocks. His moustache was grayer and, like most of us, he was heavier but his energy level had, if anything increased. He radiated enthusiasm as he unfolded the humor and drama of this page of history. There, in the newly-restored great room of the Red House Administration Building, he held us in such rapt attention that we hardly noticed the approach of twilight. Then, especially it being hunting season, the woods had become too perilous to explore on foot and we were temporarily spared another trek.

Paul started out something like this:

"My family has been coming to Allegany for forty years. I love this beautiful old place. We still come and take fourteen cabins. Somewhere during the seventies I saw this article in the paper saying there had been an Irish Village on the mountain over toward the Limestone Road. Now I'm Irish and that interested me.

"A lot of the Park people knew that New Ireland was there but they didn't know anything about who its people were, where they came from or what happened to them. So, with a friend, I started looking. It was amazing how, starting with nothing, information grew. Door after door opened for us until we had this whole story.

"We hiked in looking for New Ireland. We knew pretty much where it was but still it took the better part of half the day to find it. There, back in the woods seven-and-a-half miles from the village of Limestone, was this row of foundations along an old dirt road. We had found a Cattaraugus County map from the 1850's that named everyone in the county and located them on the map. So we had names to go with each of the foundations.

"In 1997 and '98 I was teaching an Advanced Placement History class at Cleveland Hill High School. I put them to work researching all my unanswered questions about New Ireland. It was a fortunate time since the schools had started using the internet and the students were able to use it for research and to tell the story to the public on a web page. It's still there.

"There were twelve families in New Ireland and I had twelve students. Each student took responsibility for researching a family. They were: Carmody, Carey, Fall, Hogan, Keating, Keough, McCarthy, Murphy, O'Loughlin, Parkhill, Rochford, Spellacy, Townsell and Waters.

Townsell Family Picture, New Ireland
Photo Courtesy of Paul Lewis

"The students were not Irish. They were everything else, Poles, Slavs, Italians but they took hold of this project and worked at it. They looked up census records, declarations to be come citizens and citizenship papers. They found a Patrick Que in the census and I could not for the life of me figure out who in the world he was. I got to thinking about it. Most of these folks were illiterate, couldn't write their own name. The census taker came around to each house, as they do today. He knocks on the door and inquires who lives there. Well, Patrick Keough came to the door and in his Irish brogue said (Here Paul delivered Patrick's reply in a believable brogue that I'm not quite sure how to transcribe.) 'Sure and I'm Pathrick Que.'"

Our larger-than-usual audience of fifty or more responded with an appreciative laugh.

Paul went on, "We looked up the Irish history of the 1830's and '40's. British domination had been cruel. Irish could not own land in their own country. Then potato crop failures brought on illness and death which some said was worse than the black death of the Middle Ages."

Paul illustrated his story with transparency photos by way of an overhead projector. They were cruel pictures of Irish boarding "Coffin Ships" and being crammed into the holds in their attempt to escape to the New World. They were called Coffin Ships because often 20% of the passengers died, particularly the children. The only thing for it was to throw them over the side and schools of sharks followed the ships. It took sailing ships sometimes twelve-weeks to cross the North Atlantic. The fare was only 3-5 pounds but it was usually all they had. You brought your own food.

With the pictures before us he said, "When a son, a husband or a wife left on one of these ships, those who stayed behind held an 'Irish Wake,' knowing they'd never be seen again. Those that survived the crossing were preyed upon by dockside crooks who would take the last thing they had. Yet some few of them landed up here to settle in New Ireland, and they thrived.

Paul's story made me think of my own Pierce and Beahan great grand-parents who emigrated from Ireland about this same time. They are buried in a cemetery near the deserted village of Lewisburg in Northern New York. We know very little about them or their trip over here except this one bit that has passed down to us, "We had to walk the twenty miles to board the ship in Cork."

Paul picked up with, "Now, they were Irish and most Irish are Catholic. So I took my Advanced Placement kids to Saint Patrick's Church in Limestone to see what they could find. As soon as we got inside the kids were oohing and aahing over the stained glass windows as they found windows donated by their families and with their names on them.

"The parish priest brought out old subscription lists." Paul projected an image of a list. "All our people were named on them. You could tell how they were doing. The Carmodys gave $143, one of the others families only $25. Here's the Dempseys's. I hope none of them are here today. They promised $25 and never paid. Here is a separate account for 'Woodsmen.' Guys working in the lumber mill or cutting timber would want to go to church and would throw something in the collection. They were lumped together here.

Beahan Headstone, Lewisburg Cemetery, Camp Drum

"Across the street from the church was the town History Museum. The woman in charge was a little nervous at first with all these young kids charging in but she laid out a lot of things for them, to show how life was lived in those days.

"Then we went to Saint Patrick's Cemetery. If you are an immigrant, when you are buried you want it known where you came from."

Paul flashed a photograph of Jeremiah McCarthy's gravestone on the screen. His name was clearly carved there together with the fact that he was 62 when he died and that he was born in Dunmahil, County Clare, Ireland. Most of the settlers in New Ireland came from villages in County Clare.

"So, he said, "the mystery was beginning to resolve. We knew where they came from.

The Lewisburg cemetery with all its Beahan and Pierce headstones flashed into my mind. None of them say where we came from.

Foundation still in existence at New Ireland

Then Paul said, "When I took the class in to New Ireland, we took the short way through Thunder Rocks. These were city kids not used to walking. They kept asking, 'Mister Lewis, how far is it?' They couldn't believe that these folks hiked seven miles down into Limestone every Sunday just to go to church. But the kids were thrilled when we got to the foundations of the actual homes where their families lived. They marveled at the carefully-fitted stonework that still stood without the help of cement.

For a little while on that hike I had lost four of the kids. Thank God I found them before we left or that would have been the end of this story right there.

"On some of our trips we probed with a metal rod into likely garbage sites. We found broken dishes, medicine bottles of blown glass and one high-button shoe just like we saw women wearing in some of the old pictures that the kids had turned up. I have all the pieces to one big bowl fitted together.

Paul Lewis leading ADK and the Historical Society on a tour of New Ireland on a very rainy day in October 2011

"I've wanted to store some of these relics in the Park so people could see them but the Parks are so short of cash they have never been able to do anything with them.

"We found old newspaper clippings and eventually even pictures of the buildings and of the people who lived there.

"The story that we developed was that Jeremiah McCarthy came to America on his own. He had a job on the railroad that ran from New York City to Chicago through Limestone and discovered all this vacant land for sale, cheap. He took a job in the Limestone Tannery which was then the largest sole-leather tannery in the world. He earned enough money to bring his wife, Margaret Ann, over from Ireland and to buy land for a farm up in what became New Ireland. He wrote to his friends and neighbors back home in County Clare about the land and the jobs and the fact that over here you could not only own land but you could eat meat and potatoes every day. Eleven families came to join the McCarthys. They cleared the land of trees, built houses and barns, took jobs in town and fed themselves from subsistence farms. Then of course they thrived particularly well when oil was discovered on their land. They moved to town and beyond, some as far as California."

The New Ireland story must have happened many times as Irish immigrants flooded the United States. My own great grandfather, William Henry Beahan, left County Cork for Liverpool and somehow found his way into the woods not far from Watertown, New York at a place called Sterling Bush which later became Lewisburg. There he married Roseanna Pierce, the eldest daughter of the large Pierce family who also had recently fled Ireland. Like the Keoughs who were recorded in the U.S. census as the Ques, William and Roseanna Beahan were once recorded as the Bohans.

An old Lewis County map containing Lewisburg shows the Beahans and Pierces owning homes and small farms laid out a lot like New Ireland. Up there the industry was logging and iron mining. Some of the family was in the business of burning wood into charcoal to fuel primitive blast furnaces. I've visited Lewisburg. A ruined stone blast furnace still stands there.

Like New Ireland was deserted and absorbed by Allegany, folks left Lewisburg and it was absorbed by Camp

Drum, the training ground for the Army's 10th Mountain Division. On one occasion I was visiting there with my sister and our elderly parents when a soldier in battle dress came rushing out from behind a barricade, "There is a live-fire operation going on, you've got to get out of here."

We left abruptly.

In the Historical Society meeting that preceded Paul's talk, Bob Schmid reported on the disappearance in Allegany State Park, only ten days before, of 92-year-old Reverend Thomas Hamilton. The Sheriff and hundreds of volunteers had searched for him all that time and had given it up the day of the meeting. They hoped that with deer season beginning, hunters would find him.

Bridgett Townsell and Unidentified Young Men
Photo Courtesy of Paul Lewis

In response to Bob's report, Paul told the following story: "One of the Townsell descendants out in California heard about our study of New Ireland. It was back in 1998. He must have read the website our students put together. The Townsells came east to pick up their daughter who was being discharged from the military. I arranged to meet them in Limestone. After we visited St. Patrick's, I had them in my van and we were driving up the old Limestone road into the Park. I was going on about how pristine and isolated the place was and how pleased and proud they would be at what their grandfather had accomplished. Then we came onto this crowd of police cars, pickup trucks, people on horseback, men with side arms. I couldn't believe what I saw and Mister Townsell was flabbergasted.

Townsell Family Members

"We had arrived in the middle of the search for Charlie Sheets. He was an 82-year-old Californian who had grown up in New Ireland. He was one of the Irish boys the O'Loughlin family adopted from Father Baker's in Buffalo. He remembered the village fondly and he remembered that he once buried a can of coins there. He returned with a shovel and a metal detector. Leaving his car at Thunder Rocks, he wandered into the woods and died.

"The Townsells and I," said Paul, "explored New Ireland, worried what we might find. We found their old homestead but not Charlie Sheets. Soon after that, the Sheriff located Charlie lying peacefully in the woods. Apparently he died of a heart attack.

"No one has reported finding his can of coins.

"People who have been alone up there at New Ireland have reported some strange feelings and sights. Some believe Mary McCarthy, who died there in 1860 after a house fell on her, still haunts the place.

"In any case, when we studied New Ireland it was the early days of the internet which proved very useful to us. I was able to locate an Irish website in County Clare. It had been put up by a high school principal in the town of Ennistymon. I contacted him and he put his students to work researching our New Ireland family names in parish and property records over there. They turned up a great deal of information for us. One bit that escaped all of us though was the whereabouts of the McCarthy home village of Dunmahil. No one had heard of it. I defy you to find it on a map.

"But by way of the internet, I did find an early-morning-radio host in Clare who invited our students to participate in his call-in show. The kids didn't realize they'd have to get up at 3 a.m. to be on the show, but they toughed it out. He had them on the phones each telling their New Ireland family's story. One mentioned our frustration over not finding Dunmahil. In the middle of his story, a call came in. (Paul brought out the Brogue again for this) 'Sure and I'm sittin' here in Dunmahil,' the voice over the phone said.

"Later the Irish students located a letter in the Dunmahil parish records written by John Sheehan, the parish priest in which he declared that Margaret Ann McCarthy, wife of Jeremiah McCarthy, was a respectable woman residing in that town. The letter was probably intended for immigration authorities.

Paul closed with, "From knowing nothing about the people who had lived in New Ireland we had come to know their names, what they looked like, how they lived, where they came from and what became of them."

We all applauded and Paul promised to return to lead the hikers among us back to the actual site of New Ireland.

Bob Schmid stood up right away. He, too, knows a lot about New Ireland and had probably been bursting to speak all afternoon. Only Paul's cataract of information could have held him in check. Now he burst forward to thank Paul and to put on the table a stack of the books he and Paul had jointly authored "The Legends and Lore of Allegany State Park."

Bob announced, "The New Ireland story is in our book. On the table in the back of the room, I have Xeroxes of newspaper clippings and a CD full of photographs of New Ireland for anyone who would like them."

I personally was grateful for the efforts of both these two hard-working historians but would have been even more grateful if they had mentioned my own book, "Allegany Hellbender Tales" which contains an account of New Ireland and of the Historical Society's last actual, in-person trip to the site. So I take the privilege of advertising that fact here.

After Paul had finished, people crowded around him with questions. To the surprise of us all, one couple turned out to be Murphys whose grandparents, in fact, helped to settle New Ireland. Next time we will have to hear their version of this continuing story.

More information awaits at Paul Lewis's New Ireland Website:
http://home.comcast.net/~dickallen5/nycattar/new_ireland/NI_Index.html

TUNESASSA
PETE SMALLBACK

February 2009

The Quaker Indian School at Tunesassa

A crowd of Carl Dean "Pete" Smallback's friends and relatives, most of them members of the Historical Society, turned out to hear him spin yarns about the Smallback farm. Their beautiful and historic farm was once Tunesassa, the Quaker Seneca Indian School. It is now Allegany State Park's access to Kinzua Reservoir, Friends Boat Launch.

Nobody, including Pete, knows why he is called "Pete" instead of Carl Dean. The only explanation he could offer was, "When I was a kid my dad gave me a calf to raise named Repeat." Pete is a big, tall, straight-backed ruddy-complected seventyish farmer who usually wears a faded flannel shirt and jeans. He looks like he just came in from throwing bales of hay into a loft, which may often be the case, since he still runs a dairy farm.

Pete Smallback at Tunesassa, once the Quaker Indian School Later his Family Farm

In connection with Pete's formidable size, Bob Schmid told this story. "Some high-spirited guys from Bradford had had a little too much firewater and were looking for a fight.

Pete picked up one end of an automobile and the rowdies simmered right down."

Pete had arrived early at our Historical Society meeting and spread out on the speaker's table pictures and xeroxed copies of newspaper articles about the farm. He stood patiently smiling while the unusually congested agenda of our business meeting wound down. Then Bob Schmid took the opportunity of so many old members being present to introduce almost all of them. Bob then picked up on the recent airplane disaster near Buffalo in Clarence to tell of the1951 crash of a Curtiss C-46 in the Bucktooth hills north of the Park. Pete kept smiling and finally got to speak, after a mercifully short introduction by Rick Feuz.

**Historical Society Sign in
Red House Administration Building Hallway**

Pete began the story of Tunesassa, "In 1798 the Philadelphia Quakers established a 150-acre farm along the Allegany at Old Town. The idea was to help the Senecas learn the White man's system of farming. In 1802 the Quakers moved up the Allegany a few miles to Tunesassa at Quaker Run where they bought 692 acres from the Holland Land Company. They built a gristmill and a sawmill which they used to cut lumber and grind grain for the Indians. There was rapid growth. They added a one-room schoolhouse, then a two room schoolhouse and pretty soon a boarding school. They developed farmland around the school to help support the operation. In 1886 their buildings burned down and the most recent buildings went up in 1887. The story is very well told in a book called *A Quaker Promise Kept* by Lois Barton. You can get it at Barnes and Noble.

Pete's Mom in White Sweater

"From 1900 till into the 1930s Tunesassa was one of the best farms in Cattaraugus County. First they had a herd of Jerseys and then they switched to Holsteins. It was very good productive land and the river was there to move their product to market. Then in the 1930's they had financial problems. The farm produced a lot of milk. When the creamery went out of business there was no money for upkeep. Their bills could not be paid and in '38 the school closed. The buildings continued to be used as community buildings for dances and basketball games.

"In 1944 Alfred Roberts bought the farm from the Quakers. My dad always wanted a farm. Where we lived up near Bob Banks' place he had a cow. But the cow died. Then he had some chickens. He bought two heifers and we built stalls for them out of old lumber from the Park. Finally he bought Tunesassa from Roberts, 485 acres, a house and a good barn. We had 10 cows and that January we started shipping milk. He gave me a cow but my cow died so he gave me another.

"My father was a forward-going farmer. He bought everything new. He worked all the while in the CCC Camps and on oil rigs along with running the farm. Finally he was offered full-time Electrician in the Park. Mother swept the barn floors and worked in the hay barn. I helped out.

"In '51 I liked farming and wasn't interested in college so I went to work on the farm. Dad bought the first diesel tractor around here. We rented land from the John family and others. In 1958 we put up a grass silo. I remember the first year it smelled terrible. We overhauled the barn. An old section of the barn had collapsed and three of our heifers were trapped in it. The crew from the Park came down and rescued them.

"We had cows the whole length of the barn. The milk house was way down at the far end. Every pail of milk had to be carried all the way down there to be strained."

Someone in the audience asked, "Was Tunesassa a station on the Underground Railroad?"

Pete answered, "There was a cellar under the barn. Took us two years to find it. A nice laid-up cellar. The Indians stored sugar beets down there but it could have been an Underground Railroad place for slaves to hide in. Some people said, 'How could they get across the Allegany.' Well, they got across Lake Erie.

"Surprised me how the Quakers opposed the whole country on a lot of things like slavery and never got run out of town. Even the Indians had their disagreements with them. The Quakers always wore these grey suits with white shirts. Indians wanted them, too. But when they got them they wore out in six months. The Indians didn't realize that the Quakers had a couple of suits and kept them in shape.

"The original deed was from the Holland Land Company in 1806. When we bought it from Roberts it was 496 acres. When we sold it, it was down to 467."

From the back of the room Bob Sieben, who owned land adjacent to the Smallback place said, "We bought our land from his son, Tom Roberts."

Pete said, "Edna Waters bought a portion of it, too."

Gary Lucas volunteered, "Clara Finch and her husband worked for the Quakers and they lived in the Tunesassa Cottage until '62 or 63. The bell from the school building went to Indian School Number 7. Eventually it was returned to the Quakers in Philadelphia.

Pete said, "Dad gave Bob Remington a piece of land. Bob wanted to garden. He grew celery and cantaloupe, wonderful stuff, stuff you never hear of on a farm.

Someone in the audience said, "His garden was so good because it was right alongside the cow barn."

"Mister Remington was good with tractors. He could tell when it needed an overhaul. He'd always come down and he'd know just what new parts and plugs it needed. He had a dance band, too."

Bob Sieben said, "I always remember, every time I saw you, you were putting a new engine in that '59 Chevy of yours."

"I had the '59 Chevy and Philip Attea had a '60 Convertible"

Bob interrupted, "Hook France and Al Sharpe would be sitting in a Patrol Car, see this car come racing through the Park burning up tires. Then they'd say, 'Oh, it's just Pete.' And let you pass."

Pete went on, "I came home from the service. Didn't know what I was going to do. The boss up in the Park told me to come and drive a truck. I said I didn't have a license. He said, "Don't worry about it.' In the fall I went back to work for the Power Company.

"Dad knew the Kinzua Dam was coming, so he didn't want to invest too much money in our buildings. They were planning the Dam way back in 1908. In 1924 the Army Corps did a study. In '41 Congress approved the money.

"In 1965 houses were being bought up. The people got their money and at first they were able to go out in the surrounding community and buy. But pretty soon housing became short and prices went way up. The government appraised our place and made an offer. We could not find another farm we liked so well. So along with 17 to 19 others, Dad refused. When you refused they were supposed to put 25% of the offer in the bank for you to use. In July 1965 Gerald Anderson served papers of eviction on us. But the government had not deposited the money. We had to move out and there was no money. We wrote all kinds of letters and got nowhere. Finally in 1972 Sid Shane, a lawyer from Ellicottville who worked in Salamanca, was playing golf with some state official. They got talking about the lack of payment. The State Official said, 'That's terrible.' And in 30 days we had our money. It's not what you know, it's who you know.

We moved to Steamburg and fixed up an old house to live in. We bought another one for a camp. Dad worked on the Roads from '65 to '68. Then we found the place we have now. And we decided to go after the "Big Bucks" farming. We're still looking for them. So's my son back there." He waved to his son in the audience. "He's about to inherit this mess."

Bob Sieben asked, "What caused your barn to burn?"

"Probably got torched. A lot of the places were."

"They let you buy stuff. The Park used cut stone from the foundation all through the Park. We bid on two places. Dad bought a staircase out of one. The house he built on the farm for us in the 1940's got sold. They moved it out to Steamburg or Randolph. I helped dig the new basement for it.

"The Tunesassa School Building was in beautiful shape and it was never flooded. It should have been preserved as a historic site. Some of the rubble is still there in the woods by the boat launch. There was a small cemetery with three graves, two adults and an unnamed child. The graves were moved.

Bob Schmid knew some of Pete's stories and drew them out of him with a few well-directed questions like, "Tell us about your father's quiet way of teaching you a lesson."

Pete laughed, "Phil Attea and I were out pretty late having a good time. I got home about four AM and dad said, 'Oh, you're up early ready for work, huh?' I said 'Yes.' And he worked me like a dog all day. You had to learn how to nap on your feet, so tired and hung over.

"I came in late another night in a freak snow storm. Dad and I both slept downstairs. I heard our truck start up. I woke him up and told him. He said, 'It's nothing. Go back to sleep.' But then we heard the truck going out the drive. He grabbed his rifle and we went running out. He was a marksman, could hit an 18-inch target at a thousand yards. We'd be out there shooting at woodchucks. There'd be shell casings all over the place. He'd say, 'What you shooting at?' Pick up a rifle and bang, no more woodchuck. These two guys had broke into a camp. One guy was picked up along the road, the other stole our truck. Dad could have shot him. The police knew he was coming and stopped him a little way down.

"Dorothy and Ken Carnahan bought the farm next to us. She had been a housemaid in Wolf Run. Six days a week she'd cook in the lumber camp back there.

"The Jansen family ran a leather goods store in Buffalo. They used to come down on weekends and tent camp. They would have breakfast with us. Dad sold them 16 acres for their own camp.

"The Ritz family, back up in Wolf Run, used to have these six-foot rattlesnake skins nailed up to their barn door. The foundation of the place was still there ten years ago. Every year they'd drive down into the Park with a box of rattlers covered with a screen. The Park used to try to keep quiet about rattlers. Once, at the Fancher Pool in Quaker, something went wrong with the electric system. These two great big Park workers went into the pump house to check on it. One of them reached up onto a high shelf; felt a snake and the two of them came flying out. It was a dead rattler that had crawled in there and got fried shorting it out.

"There still are some snakes around. On a warm summer day, in dry weather I'd be careful camping along the Kinzua." With that, Rick Feuz gave Pete a plaque depicting the Red House Covered Bridge and the rest of us gave Pete a big hand while the crowd moved up front to congratulate him and look through all the documents and photos he had brought along.

PART FOUR

POLITICS

MINERAL RIGHTS SUNSET LAW

April 2010

Gas Well Just Inside the Pennsylvania Border at the Top of Allegany's Black Snake Nature Trail

This is a memorandum of support prepared by Roger Downs of the Sierra Club's Atlantic Chapter. <u>The bill sponsored by Assemblyman Sam Hoyt and Senator Dale Volker is now law.</u> It is intended to deal with the problem that mineral rights under half of Allegany State Park are privately owned and if they were exercised it would mean the destruction of much of the forest.

Sierra Club
Memorandum of Support

A.9070) Hoyt / (S.7170) Volker

Title: An act to amend the real property law, in relation to lapse of oil and gas interests in Allegany State Park

Purpose: To protect the fragile, rare and important forest ecosystem of Allegany State Park from the disruption of oil and gas exploration.

Summary: Amends the Real Property Law by adding a new section 329-a to provide that oil and gas interests in Allegany State Park unused for 20 years will lapse and revert to New York State unless a statement of claim is filed by the owner of the mineral interest prior to the end of the 20-year period prior to the effective date or within two years of the effective date of this statute whichever is later. Failure to file a statement of claim will not result in lapse if a statement is filed within 60 days of the publication of notice of lapse by the original owner or within 60 days of actual knowledge of the lapse.

Justification:
Allegany State Park, the largest of NY's State Parks is 67,000 acres of 100 to 350 year-old forest of a quality and type that is rare in NY State. When the Park was put together in 1921, it was done quickly and imperfectly. As a result half the mineral rights under the Park are privately owned and their owners are extremely difficult to determine and to locate. If these

rights were exercised it would result in unacceptable disruption of this exemplary forest system.

The recent discovery of the availability of natural gas in the Marcellus Shale under the Park make recovery of these mineral rights a matter of urgency. The Mega-hydrofracturing and horizontal drilling of wells with 5-acre wellheads, heavy truck traffic and water contamination that is necessary to tap this store of gas is particularly destructive to surface ecology and totally inappropriate in a Park setting .

The Sierra Club Atlantic Chapter believes that it is essential to the integrity of Allegany State Park that every effort possible is made to see that there is no further gas or oil exploration there. It is a first priority of our organization to see that A9070 and S70110 are enacted into law.

A NEW ALLEGANY MASTER PLAN

April 2010

Allegany State Park has been without a Master Plan to guide its administrators for many years. <u>This plan which provides for indispensable protections to Allegany's forest, wildlife, geology and streams, balanced with reasonable provisions for recreation is finally in effect.</u> Roger Downs wrote this memorandum:

Bruce Kershner Leading the Historical Society into the Now-protected Big Basin Hemlock Old Growth Forrest

Sierra Club
Memorandum of Support

Draft Master Plan/ Draft Environmental Impact Statement for Allegany State Park announced April 14, 2010

Title of Action:
Adoption and Implementation of a Master Plan for Allegany State Park

SEQR Status:
Type I

Location of Action: Allegany State Park is located in the Towns of Red House, Carrollton, Cold Spring, South Valley, Salamanca, and Great Valley in Cattaraugus County.

Purpose: To present for public comment a draft plan designed to guide the stewardship of the resources at Allegany State Park. The Park's exemplary 100 to 350-year-old forest has in recent years been threatened with lumbering and more recently with disruption by Marcellus Shale gas exploration.

Summary:
The goal of the Draft Master Plan for Allegany State Park is to keep it a place for the public to visit, enjoy and appreciate the natural, cultural and physical resources and the recreational opportunities that the Park offers and to achieve a balance between recreational use and the protection of the biological, physical and cultural resources of the Park.

The plan will guide the Park:

To provide a diversity of high quality recreation opportunities balanced with stewardship of the Park's natural and cultural resources.

To identify, protect and interpret the natural resources of the Park.

To develop, maintain and operate high quality facilities, recreation opportunities and programs that are consistent with both the recreational needs of the patrons and the character of Park resources.

To identify, preserve, protect and interpret important historic, archaeological and cultural resources.

To protect and maintain the scenic quality of the Park, its vistas, landscapes and views of natural areas from adverse visual impacts from both outside and within the Park.

Continue to protect open space within the legislated boundary and adjacent to the Park through acquisition consistent with the *2009 New York State Open Space Conservation Plan*, and through coordination of stewardship with partners.

Draft Plan elements:
The elements of the plan that will accomplish these goals are available at http://www.nysparks.com/inside-our-agency/public-documents.aspx

New designations of the Park: Chief among these elements and crucial to them are the designations of the Park as a "Natural Heritage Area," "Bird Conservation Area" and 85% of it as "Park Preserve." Park Preserve status offers Allegany the same "Forever Wild" protection as the Old Growth Forest in Zoar Valley and the Forest Preserve in the Adirondacks. These new designations will make it possible for the State to reject proposals for gas and oil exploration in the Park on environmental grounds and, in that way, give the State time to acquire the privately owned mineral rights under the Park.

Trails: The proposed trail system is thoughtful, diversified and technically well laid out. However, the Plan proposes an expansion of trail system mileage from 148 to 227 miles. Sierra Club raises the question "Does this additional trail mileage tilt the balance too much toward recreation and away from resource protection?" The proposed increased mileage will be difficult to maintain. The current trail system in the Park has suffered lack of maintenance. The additional trails would interrupt the continuity of more of the forest and the additional traffic would lessen its usefulness as wildlife habitat.

Sierra urges OPRHP planners to consider a less elaborate expansion of the trail system.

Justification:

Allegany State Park, established in 1921, is the largest of NY's State Parks. Its 67,000 acres of 100 to 350-year-old forest is of a quality and type that is rare in NY State. The Park is open year-round and hosts approximately 1.5 million visitors annually.

The Park's geology is unique for being non-glaciated. This distinction influences the soils, surface geology, topography and flora and fauna of the Park. There are areas of the Park which have been virtually undisturbed since its establishment and in some cases, for many years before that. This has allowed vast stretches of forest to mature with little or no intervention other than the impacts of natural processes. Because of this, many of the ecological communities that have developed in the Park during this time are either rare or are of significance because of their high quality. Wildlife is abundant with many species of birds, fish, mammals, reptiles and amphibians.

Camping, cabins and cottages are available for overnight visitors. Swimming, hiking, bicycling, horseback riding, skiing, snowshoeing, snowmobiling, picnicking, hunting, fishing, and nature studies are all available at the Park as well as opportunities to simply relax and enjoy scenic beauty.

When the Park was put together in 1921, it was done quickly and imperfectly. As a result, half the mineral rights under the Park are still privately owned and their owners are extremely difficult to determine and to locate. If these rights were exercised it would result in unacceptable disruption of the Park and its exemplary forest system.

A 100-year-old Allegany black cherry safe for another 100 years

The recent discovery of the availability of natural gas in the Marcellus Shale under the Park makes recovery of these mineral rights a matter of urgency. The high-volume hydrofracturing and horizontal drilling of wells with 5-acre wellheads, heavy truck traffic and water contamination necessary to tap this store of gas would be particularly destructive to surface ecology and totally inappropriate in a park.

Conclusion: The Sierra Club Atlantic Chapter applauds the OPRHP crew that put together this excellent and much needed Draft Allegany State Park Master Plan so quickly and so well. We heartily recommend approval of the plan with the one recommendation that the expansion of the trail system be dialed back to restore balance between resource preservation and recreation.

Made in the USA
Lexington, KY
22 October 2012